The Chicanos

Life and Struggles of the Mexican Minority in the United States

by Gilberto López y Rivas

With Readings

Translated and edited by
Elizabeth Martínez and
Gilberto López y Rivas

Monthly Review Press
New York and London

*To the Chicano people of the United States,
as a contribution to their just struggle*

Originally published as *Los Chicanos: una
minoria nacional explotada* by Editorial
Nuestro Tiempo, Mexico, copyright © 1971
by Editorial Nuestro Tiempo, S.A.

Library of Congress Cataloging in Publication Data
Lopez y Rivas, Gilberto.
   The Chicanos: life and struggles of the Mexican
minority in the United States.
   Bibliography: p.
   1. Mexican Americans. I. Title.
E184.M5L613   301.45′16′872073   73–8056
ISBN 0–85345–298–9

First Printing

Monthly Review Press
116 West 14th Street, New York, N.Y. 10011
33/37 Moreland Street, London, E.C. 1

Manufactured in the United States of America

Contents

Introduction to the English-Language Edition: A Word to My Fellow Anthropologists

Many years have passed since anthropology freed itself from an orthodoxy of subject matter. More and more we find that the once rigid boundary lines of all the disciplines of the social sciences are giving way under the pressure of new fields of investigation, in the search for answers to questions posed by complex and multifaceted problems. The profound techno-economic, social, and political changes which have taken place in this century; the breaking-up of the colonial system and the establishment of imperialism; the emergence of socialism; the struggles of people for liberation from economic and political domination; the incorporation of traditional societies as national states—all these developments have provoked a revision in the methodology and subject matter of social science in general, and of anthropology in particular.

Thus we can say that the study of so-called primitive peoples—that old hunting ground of ethnographic collectors—has gradually changed to an analysis of urban and industrialized societies, of the problems of the big centers of world power, and of the rural and urban areas of countries ruled by those centers. In other words, anthropology has been extended from its former concern with native groups in colonized areas to questions raised by complex contemporary societies and the new relationships within the imperialist domain. As Peter Worsley has pointed out, anthropology faces the dilemma of maintaining its traditional preoccupation with the primitive and inevitably dying, along with its objects of study, or broadening its field of interest and investigation.[1]

It cannot be said often enough that anthropology as a science was born with an original sin from which it has not yet received complete absolution. Anthropology was organized and developed as a tool of colonialism; the study of non-European peoples was saturated with the needs of colonial administrators. As Claude Lévi-Strauss has commented:

> Anthropology is not a dispassionate science like astronomy, which originates in the contemplation of faraway things. It is the result of a historic process which has made the greater part of humanity subject to the other part, and in the course of which millions of human beings have seen their natural resources disappear through exploitation, their institutions and beliefs destroyed, while they themselves have been brutally murdered, enslaved, and infected with diseases they could not resist.[2]

Unfortunately, the process that Lévi-Strauss describes has changed only in its methods and we still find many anthropologists and other scientists offering their services to programs whose concrete purposes lie in the areas of political and economic control and military repression. We can recall, for example, the "Camelot" plan, studies made in Vietnam and Thailand, the close relationship between certain U.S. universities and the Defense Department, the CIA, etc.

At the same time, anthropology has not lacked men and women who have devoted their professional lives to better causes than defending exploitation. The most strongly based refutations of racism and ethnocentrism have come from the ranks of anthropologists; numerous voices have been raised to denounce oppressive conditions and the systematic extermination of the world's "native" peoples. Keeping alive this tradition of social commitment, some anthropologists from the imperialist centers, as well as the most progressive social scientists of the Third World, have made a commitment to the oppressed and decided not to continue being accomplices of exploitation. A group of young Mexican anthropologists has stated:

> For us the important task is not to accumulate facts and anecdotes, nor to catalogue "exotic" ways of life, as did the classical anthropologists in their condescending liberalism. . . . For us, the main task is not transforming the mentality of the oppressed but changing the situation which oppresses them. We ask for a way of thinking and understanding society from the viewpoint of the needs, interests, and concrete lives of the marginal, exploited, and colonized peoples of the world.[3]

From all these ideas—the ferment of my years of academic preparation—has emerged my interest in the subject of this book. In publishing this English edition, we recognize the special reasons for presenting the problem of the Chicanos.

First, we believe that the expansion of the United States at the expense of native groups has frequently been seen as a "natural" result of a confrontation between the Anglo and groups of people considered to be destined by "providential design" to be conquered, exploited, and exterminated. The conflicts between the "colonizer" and the American Indians, between the "frontiersman" and the Mexicano, between the Anglo and the Chicano, have been presented as a clashing of races resulting from purely biological necessity—as a clear example of the supposed fact that, in the struggle for survival, the strongest has the absolute right to triumph over his enemies regardless of moral questions and of the price or the means used. The purest kind of "social Darwinism" has filled those pages of history books telling us about the "heroic" struggles of the pioneers who colonized the West.

In U.S. history, the "winning of the West" has been beautified and idealized into a crusade carried out by men who were brave and democratic (although "individualistic") to civilize the West—forgetting what that conquest meant for the original inhabitants of those lands. Out of egocentricity, the North American has seen only himself in this tragedy that settled the destiny of many people. The "frontier"—the West—meant adventure, courage, self-confidence, and independence for Lyndon B. Johnson,[4] but for the Indian and the Mexican, that same frontier has meant cultural elimination, land robbery, death, and submission. For Johnson, the frontier developed an important instinct in the Anglo—"an instinct to preserve the equality of opportunity, the dignity of the individual, the commitment to justice for all. . . ."[5] But the Indian and the Mexican can give proof that this "instinct" has been, up to now, one of the purest ethnocentricity, the most stubborn racism.

In a book written by a man who was president of the American Historical Association in 1958, with a foreword by an ex-president of the United States, and published by a U.S. university, we can read such statements as this: "The language is Spanish, or Mexican, the religion Catholic, the temperament volatile and mercurial. Without disparagement it may be said that there is a cruel streak in the Mexican nature. . . . This cruelty may be a heritage from the Spanish of the Inquisition; it may, and doubtless should, be attributed partly to the Indian blood."[6]

Such statements abound in publications which, one can assume, have a certain academic seriousness. Actually, we should not be surprised to find such racist mentalities within the camp of social science. We know that social science has not been, and is not, free from the ideological, philosophical, or political conflicts which divide our world, despite all the claims of dedication to "pure science."

Another stereotype inspired by the mythology of U.S. racism has been the idea that the Mexican in the conquered territories received Anglo rule with open arms. It has been assumed that the history of the so-called Mexican-American was characterized by total submissiveness—until the Chicano movement suddenly emerged in the 1960s. This is a false idea, and we affirm that the spirit of popular resistance did not come out of the blue; that the Chicano people have a tradition and a continuity of social struggle against outside rulers. This book, like many other studies made by Chicano social scientists, is presented with the goal of changing that deformed image of the Mexicano in the United States, and trying to hammer out the true, combative reality of a people who, from the very moment of being conquered, could express their dissatisfaction and preserve their dignity, sometimes with bullets, sometimes with the popular stanzas of a *corrido*, and almost always with a firm determination to continue the culture, language, and traditions which the land of Mexico bequeathed to them.

Notes

1. Peter Worsley, *The End of Anthropology? Actes du sixième congrès mondial de sociologie* (Belgium, 1966).
2. Claude Lévi-Strauss, as quoted by Gutorm Gjessing in "La Responsabilidad Social del Científico Social," *America Indigena* (Mexico), vol. 29, no. 3 (1969), p. 823.
3. Grupo de los Viernes (The Friday Group), "Acerca de la Antropología Militante." Mimeographed. Escuela Nacional de Antropología e Historia, Mexico, 1969. See also Theodore Roszak, ed., *The Dissenting Academy* (New York: Pantheon, 1967), and relevant articles in *América Indigena* (Mexico), vol. 23, no. 3, 1969.

4. Lyndon B. Johnson, Foreword to Walter Webb, *The Texas Rangers* (Austin, Tex.: University of Texas Press, 1970).
5. Ibid., p. x.
6. Webb, *The Texas Rangers*, p. 14.

I

The Chicanos

Introduction

It seems that a long-standing situation of social injustice is "discovered" only after there has been a violent reaction from the oppressed group, or when it appears "dangerously explosive"—even though the situation is always obvious to anyone who is not in the oppressor's camp.

Thus the problem of the Chicanos—Mexican-Americans, people of Mexican origin in the United States—suddenly exploded as the result of newspaper headlines. It fell upon Reies Lopez Tijerina, leader of the Alianza Federal de los Pueblos Libres (Federal Alliance of Free Peoples), to act as detonator.* It was he who, in the 1960s, focused attention on the Chicano's long history of discrimination and misery. It was he who brought to light what has been called "one of the United States' best-kept secrets."

Yet the "secret" had long been known to all who took part in the Chicano people's struggle to defend those rights which were theoretically granted them in 1848 by the Treaty of Guadalupe Hidalgo. That treaty, signed at the end of the

---

* The event was the widely publicized "courthouse raid" of June 5, 1967, when a group of armed men took over a county courthouse in northern New Mexico to pursue their struggle for land and justice. The men were all members of the Alianza and were led by Reies Lopez Tijerina, who had often spoken out against the oppression of the Chicano.

United States' war on Mexico, guaranteed the right of all Mexicans who stayed in the seized territories to maintain their culture, their lands, their language, and their political rights. More than a century has gone by since then and the history of the Chicanos has been one of constant, systematic, and increasing violation not only of all the treaty promises but also of the most basic human rights as set down by the United Nations in its Universal Declaration of Human Rights of 1948.

In 1959 a petition was presented to the United Nations by a group of U.S. citizens asking for a thorough investigation of the treatment Mexicans receive in the United States.[1] The petition pointed out that people of Mexican origin or from Mexican families suffer discrimination based on race, color, language, national origin, and political opinions. The petition denounced the violation of those articles in the Declaration of Human Rights which guarantee life, liberty, and personal safety; those dealing with freedom to choose an occupation, as well as the right to favorable working conditions and equal pay for equal labor; those which prohibit arbitrary arrest, detention, or exile, decree equal protection under the law, and affirm the right to citizenship.

The petition provided a brief glimpse at the conditions under which the Mexican minority—then five million people, according to the petition—lives. The full, daily reality of a social crime can never be adequately described by any document, no matter how precise.

One group which has helped keep the long silence about a situation affecting the lives of millions of human beings is those whom some Chicanos have called "scientific mercenaries." These are the sociologists and anthropologists dedicated to research that hides and distorts the true conditions of the society under study, and imposes on it the ideological values of the dominant group. Thus we find ourselves confronted by many studies of Chicanos that seldom touch on the socioeconomic foundations of their lives.

Our awareness of this situation led to the idea of writing a short book that would contribute to a better understanding of the Mexican-American's oppression. We decided to make such a study, not because it is "interesting"—as those who look upon social science like avid collectors of strange phenomena would describe it—but because it represents one more example of the human suffering caused by the same system that makes exploitation and injustice possible in our own country, Mexico.

It is important to point out that we have attempted only to present certain aspects of the living conditions of Mexican people in the United States. Our desire has been to pose the problem as a basis for future research projects in which the questions raised here may be of interest. It has not at any time been our intention to arrive at definite statements or conclusions about the Mexican people in the United States, but rather to stimulate the discussion and controversy which are inseparable from scientific dialogue.

Notes

1. *A Badge of Infamy: A Petition to the United Nations on the Treatment of the Mexican Immigrant* (New York: American Committee for the Protection of Foreign Born, 1959).

1
Some Historical Background

From the beginning of its history as a nation, the United States planned territorial, economic, and political expansion at the expense of the "backward" Spanish colonies in America. The leaders of the United States themselves confirmed this: in 1786 Thomas Jefferson expressed his fear that Spain might not be able to hold its dominions in America until the population was numerous enough to take them over, section by section. And Henry Clay dreamed as early as 1811 of the United States expanding across the American continent from the Arctic Ocean to South America. These attitudes do not reflect the opinions of isolated individuals; rather, they must be seen as expressing the goals of the social class to which those men belonged—the ruling class.

History has shown that when the ruling classes decide on conquest as a means of establishing their domination over others there is always an upsurge of ideas and theories to justify such acts of plunder, to beautify and glorify them. Usually these ideas are based on an absolute belief in one's own superiority, in being a "chosen" people, who bear the burden ("divine mission") of deciding human destinies.

At the beginning of the nineteenth century, there existed in the United States a certainty that this country was the "nation chosen by Providence" to watch over the well-being of the whole continent. Assurance of strong economic development lay the foundation for a belief in racial superiority, a contempt for inferior races, and a firm conviction in the duty to save "savage" peoples from misery and ignorance. In the 1830s these ideas were given the subtle name of "Manifest Destiny" and became the basis of U.S. foreign policy—as they are today.

During the 1846–1848 war of aggression against Mexico, Sam Houston exclaimed: "The Anglo-Saxon race must pervade the whole southern extremity of this vast continent . . . The Mexicans are no better than the Indians and I see no reason why we should not . . . take their land . . . We are now in this war . . . giving peace, security, and happiness to those oppressed people." President Theodore Roosevelt would later say that the United States' manifest destiny was to absorb the territory of the neighboring nations that were too weak to oppose this.

The doctrine of Manifest Destiny and the so-called Monroe Doctrine are the two ideological pillars of North American interventionism in the young Latin American nations. The difference between the two lies in the fact that the first was an open announcement of the U.S. government's plans, while the second lent itself better to concealing the true purposes of a budding imperialism. But the desire for imperialist expansion was and is the common denominator of Manifest Destiny and the Monroe Doctrine.

Frederick Merk, in his book, *Manifest Destiny and Mission in American History*, sums up the fundamental principles of this ideology as it was expressed in the speeches and press of the 1840s:

It [Manifest Destiny] meant expansion, prearranged by Heaven, over an area not clearly defined. In some minds it meant expansion over the region to the Pacific; in others, over the North American continent; in others, over the hemisphere. . . . It meant opportunity to gain admission to the American Union. Any neighboring people, established in self-government by compact or by successful revolution, would be permitted to apply. If properly qualified, they would be admitted. *Some—the Mexican, for example—might have to undergo schooling for a time in the meaning and methods of freedom before they were let in.* A century might be necessary to complete the structure of the great American nation of the future. Any hurried admission to the temple of freedom would be unwise; any forced admission would be a contradiction in terms, unthinkable, revolting. But a duty lay on the people of the United States to admit all qualified applicants freely. The doors of the temple must be wide open to peoples who were panting for freedom.[1]

The spirit of the age could not be better expressed. We can almost foresee certain events, including the Anglo-Saxon occupation of Texas and California in order to provoke a convenient "revolution" that would lead to aggression against Mexico. The spirit is not only that of North American expansionism, but also that of cultural and racial ethnocentrism, the very roots of racism, implanted with the first contact between the "frontiersmen" and the American Indians, with the arrival of the first shipload of Black Slaves.

Abraham Lincoln, historic symbol of racial justice, was capable of saying:

> I have no purpose to introduce political and social equality between the white and the black races. There is a physical difference between the two, which in my judgment will probably forever forbid their living together upon the footing of perfect equality, and inasmuch as it becomes a necessity that there must be a difference, I . . . am in favor of the race to which I belong, having the superior position.

If Lincoln could say that, then what can we expect from the avowed believers in Manifest Destiny?

The "theoretician of the doctrine" was John L. O'Sullivan, editor of the *Democratic Review* and the *New York Evening News* until 1846. He coined the phrase "Manifest Destiny" in an editorial on the Texas issue in the *Democratic Review* of July–August 1845, and in a later editorial in the *New York Evening News* defended the United States' "true title" to Oregon:

> Away, away with all these cobweb tissues of rights of discovery, exploration, settlement, contiguity, etc. . . . [The American claim] is by the right of our manifest destiny to overspread and to possess the whole of the continent which Providence has given us for the development of the great experiment of liberty. . . . It is a right such as that of the tree to the space of air and earth suitable for the full expansion of its principle and destiny of growth—such as that of the stream to the channel required for the still accumulating volume of its flow.[2]

With such statements being published in daily newspapers in the 1840s, and the coming to power of such a man as the pro-slavery President James Polk in 1845, the fate of Mexico was sealed. After the U.S. occupied Louisiana in 1803, Florida in 1819, Oregon and the territories that now comprise the states of Washington, Idaho, and parts of Wyoming and Montana in 1846, it could be expected that the air and land of Mexico would be necessary for the full growth of the hungry Yankee "tree." The war of conquest became imminent.

Mexico and the United States Before the War

Ideological positions are basically an expression of the economic processes of any given society: the dominant ideology reflects the class interests of the groups in power. Thus the vigorous economic development of the United States and the ambition of those who wielded political power there were expressed in the statements of Manifest Destiny and the Monroe Doctrine. The basis of those two ideological declarations was the idea of obtaining territories that would furnish abundant raw materials—rich land for cultivation, forests and mines, the necessary manpower. The goal was to open new markets for ever growing production and to give industry new perspectives. Expansion became the "natural" way to reach this goal. Incorporating new geographic areas not only made more buying and selling possible, but resources—especially labor—could be turned into objects for trade.

In the early 1800s the United States was preparing the ground for intervention in Latin America by conquering markets and investments, by substituting itself wherever possible for British colonialism. The United States was aware of the vast riches that existed in Mexico, not only in natural resources but also in potential human labor for the development of the U.S. economy. The inhabitants of the lands that the Yankees conquered would soon become, along with Black slaves, a part of the most exploited social group. It was felt in the United States that the "backward" Mexicans would make good yoke-oxen to break ground in the inhospitable but coveted lands of the West.

In those same years, industrial capitalism was developing rapidly in the United States; first light industry—especially textiles—and then the beginnings of heavy industry, accompanied by mass production. The historical conditions necessary to make possible a rapid accumulation of capital were present; use of a policy of force would do the rest.[3]

Next door to this scene of full capitalistic evolution, Mexico found itself in a dismal situation. The movement which had brought independence from Spain in 1821 had not greatly changed internal economic relations. Exploitation of the land still rested with the owners of huge estates, considerably enlarged by lands belonging to Indian communities. Members of these communities were becoming part of the big haciendas as *peones*, laborers; they constituted half the population of eight million.

Mexico was also in the hands of foreign capital, as a result of innumerable government loans at exorbitant interest rates, mostly from England. Almost the only industry of any importance was mining, and it was largely in foreign hands. Many Mexicans were occupied in handicrafts and grouped in trade unions of a medieval type that allowed no development of the industry.

To this precarious economic situation were added anarchy and political instability, the products of frequent uprisings and military coups. The bourgeois elements were still too weak to overcome the clergy, who owned half the land, and the other powerful landowners. The chaotic political situation was compounded by the personal ambitions of adventurers and other unscrupulous individuals.

The first decades of Mexico's history as an independent nation were characterized by a conflict between the Centralists and the Federalists. As one author explained it:

> The Centralists defended the interests of the feudal landowners, the high clergy, and the military caste. They wanted, by means of a centralized government, to guarantee the domination of the aforesaid reactionary powers over the Mexican people. The Federalists, on the other hand, supported by the nascent bourgeoisie, the liberal landowners and public functionaries, the body of officers, and the vanguard intelligentsia, demanded increased autonomy of the states, restriction of the power of the military castes and of the clergy, and the application of bourgeois reforms.[4]

Under these conditions, Mexico was inevitably hard pressed to organize for self-defense in the face of numerous U.S. actions aimed at provoking war.

The War of Conquest (1846 to 1847)

On March 1, 1845, the United States resolved to annex Texas; in December of that year Congress declared Texas incorporated as a state. This act was more than a provocation; it constituted an unofficial declaration of war. The only thing lacking was a pretext. President Polk then sent General Zachary Taylor to invade Mexican territory. On March 28, 1846, Taylor reached the left bank of the Río Bravo (Río Grande) and a month later finally found the eagerly awaited pretext: Mexican forces were accused of aggression for attacking a Yankee detachment on Mexican territory. (As if it were not an established right to repel the invasion of armed forces from a foreign country!) On May 11, the U.S. Congress issued a decree recognizing a state of war with Mexico, and the president issued a Proclamation of War on May 13.

It is unnecessary to review here the details of the outrageous aggression suffered by our people. It is enough to remember that, as in all wars of conquest, the invading army attacked with cruelty and sadism. There was no crime, no outrage, that was not committed. The feats of the U.S. troops shamed even their own leaders; General Winfield Scott admitted willingly that they had "committed atrocities to make Heaven weep and every American of Christian morals blush for his country. Murder, robbery, and rape of mothers and daughters in the presence of tied-up males of the families have been common." Lieutenant George G. Meade said that the volunteer soldiers were "driving husbands out of houses and raping their wives. They will fight as valiantly as any men, but they are a set of Goths and Vandals without discipline, making us a terror of innocent people." [5]

Such North American historians as Hubert Bancroft and Abiel Livermore have also described the invasion. Bancroft stated that the bombing of Veracruz lasted four days and was entirely unnecessary, while Livermore related that the injured were finished off on the battlefield and prisoners were burned alive. The pro-slavery press incited its readers to genocide, he said, and quoted from that press: "Unless we distress the Mexicans, carry destruction and loss of life to every fireside, and make them feel a rod of iron, they will not respect us," said one newspaper, while another maintained that if Santa Ana held out "it will be time for our government to resort to the severest measures in order to make the war tell upon the population. It is to be hoped that our army will then forage on the enemy, lay every town and hamlet through which it passes under heavy contribution." [6]

This was how the United States set out to put eight million human beings through a period of "schooling" on "the meaning and methods of freedom" so that they could be admitted into that longed-for "temple of freedom."

We must also point out the heroic resistance of the Mexican patriots against the invader. Mexican guerrillas and patriotic elements of the regular army fought with courage and audacity in spite of betrayal by the clerical and landowning groups who refused to support the resistance war. Many of those groups carried on shameful dealings with the enemy. The Catholic Church in particular did not hesitate to cooperate actively with the North Americans, rather than risk losing their large holdings by helping to finance the defense: "When the invaders were heading for the capital of the Republic, by way of Puebla, some hierarchs of the diocese of that city . . . entered into arrangements with the enemy to facilitate access to the Valley of Mexico, precisely at the moment when the national resistance—organized with such difficulty—creaked lugubriously and seemed to be falling apart." [7]

Mexico lost the war mainly because U.S. economic development made that country better armed and prepared. The United States had a well-paid and well-supplied professional army, with the most modern weapons of the times—breech-loading rifles and artillery. Mexico, on the other hand, had no regular army, its weapons were outdated, and the soldiers did not have adequate military instruction and often went unpaid. Furthermore, the groups in the United States which favored territorial expansion had been planning the aggression for a long time. This gave them the initiative in war. Mexico was torn by internal strife and its leaders put their class interests ahead of preparation for war. It was impossible to present a united and popular front to the enemy—unlike the very different circumstances of the French invasion years later.

The Treaty of Guadalupe Hidalgo

Once the invading army had occupied the capital, Mexico City, and Mexico's ability to defend itself had been nullified, it became necessary to legalize the illegality. A peace treaty was needed to sanction the United States' acquisition of Mexican territory. Mexico's delegates to the treaty negotiations wrote their government that the negotiations were simply to put the final results of the military campaign into written form. Since it had been a war of conquest, it was natural that the vanquished should be made to accept any "agreements" that the victors, guns in hand, should desire.

It is only fair to say that the Mexican delegates did everything in their power to obtain some advantages in the wake of disaster. In the first negotiations, before Mexico City was taken, U.S. voracity demanded Texas, New Mexico, and both Californias; considerable territory in the northern Mexican states of Tamaulipas, Coahuila, Chihuahua, and Sonora; and free transit across the Isthmus of Tehuantepec in southern Mexico. The rejection of those demands led to a renewal of hostilities and the taking of Mexico City. Negotiations were reopened on January 2, 1848, at the villa of Guadalupe Hidalgo, where they lasted for a month.

The final treaty, signed on February 2, spelled out an "agreement" in which Mexico lost 45 percent of its territory —916,945 square miles that included the immense riches of the Texas oil fields and the California gold areas, as well as more than 100,000 people. All this the United States took for $15 million, which was not even paid in cash. Seldom in history has a country been robbed of so much by a war.

One of the questions that most worried the Mexican

delegates at Guadalupe Hidalgo was the exiled population in the captured territories. This concern was defined in Articles VIII and IX of the treaty, which read:

Article VIII
Rights of Mexicans Established in
Territories Ceded to United States

Mexicans now established in territories previously belonging to Mexico, and which remain for the future within the limits of the United States, as defined by the present treaty, shall be free to continue where they now reside, or to remove at any time to the Mexican republic, retaining the property which they possess in the said territories, or disposing thereof, and removing the proceeds wherever they please, without their being subjected on this account to any contribution, tax, or charge whatever.

Those who shall prefer to remain in the said territories may either retain the title and rights of Mexican citizens, or acquire those of citizens of the United States. But they shall be under obligation to make their election within one year from the date of the exchange of ratifications of this treaty; and those who shall remain in the said territories after the expiration of that year, without having declared their intention to retain the character of Mexicans, shall be considered to have elected to become citizens of the United States.

In the said territories, property of every kind, now belonging to Mexicans not established there, shall be inviolably respected. The present owners, the heirs of these, and all Mexicans who may hereafter acquire said property by contract, shall enjoy with respect to it guaranties equally ample as if the same belonged to citizens of the United States.

Article IX
How Mexicans Remaining in Ceded
Territories May Become Citizens
of the United States

Mexicans who, in the territories aforesaid, shall not preserve the character of the Mexican republic, conformably with what is stipulated in the preceding article, shall be incorporated in the Union of the United States, and be admitted at the proper time (to be judged of by the Congress of the United States) to the enjoyment of all the rights of citizens of the United States, according to the principles of the Constitution; and in the meantime shall be maintained and protected in the free enjoyment of their liberty and property, and secured in the free exercise of their religion without restriction.

At one point there was also an Article X, which stated:

All grants of land made by the Mexican government, or by the competent authorities, in territories previously appertaining to Mexico, and remaining for the future within the limits of the United States, shall be respected as valid, to the same extent that the same grants would be valid if the said territories had remained within the limits of Mexico.

This article was strongly opposed by interests in the United States because it would interfere with the land-grabbing that had already taken place in Texas, New Mexico, and California—not to mention future expansion. The United States therefore threatened to start the war again if Mexico insisted on Article X. This "diplomacy" of force and threats ended with Mexico agreeing. But a protocol was signed on May 26, 1848, by the Mexican Minister of Foreign Relations and a U.S. representative, which promised that the deletion of Article X did not mean the land grants would not be respected.

The limited protection obtained for the Mexicans living in the territories taken by the United States soon proved to be of little value. They found themselves at the mercy of the new owners. The "solemn covenants" to prevent the people living in the conquered territories from suffering as a conquered people soon became dead words to a government which throughout its long history has respected only the law of its own power. With the signing of the Treaty of Guadalupe Hidalgo, the principles of which were violated only a few days afterward, the history of *los Chicanos*—"our brothers who were sold"—officially begins.[8]

A Brief History of the Conquered Lands

The territories seized by the United States had been the northern provinces of New Spain before they became part of Mexico. The Spanish conquerors, in their avid search for quick wealth through the discovery of gold and silver, began to explore the area in the early 1500s. In 1598, Juan de Oñate—who had become rich through silver mining in the state of Zacatecas—organized a large expedition to what is now the state of New Mexico. He invaded the lands of the Pueblo Indians and built a series of settlements. These were wiped out when the Indians rebelled in 1680, but twelve years later Diego de Vargas reconquered the area and laid the foundations for colonization.

In Arizona, the first centers of colonization were established by the Jesuit cartographer and chronicler, Father Eusebio Kino. In 1687 he founded the Mission Nuestra Señora de los Dolores in Sonora, south of what is now Tucson, although nomadic Indians prevented any kind of stable colonization. In Texas, the Spanish also faced perpetual resistance from nomadic Indians and only managed to settle around some Catholic missions near the Río Bravo. The coast of California was extensively colonized with missions and eventually there were twenty-one, protected by four presidios or garrisons—at San Diego, Santa Barbara, Monterey, and San Francisco.

Thus two centers of power—the military and the Church—combined to form the basis of Spanish colonization. In all, the territory under Spanish dominion consisted of a firm foundation in New Mexico, a series of missions and garrisons along the California coast, and a number of constantly endangered settlements in Texas and Arizona.

On their arrival in what became New Spain, the European

conquerors found aboriginal cultures in different stages of development. (We are speaking here about Mexico and the southwestern United States as a single area, as they were until the U.S. takeover of 1848.) The conquerors found what have been called "two native Mexicos"—one sedentary and more highly developed, the other nomadic and found mostly in the north. Once the bloody process of military submission was over, the Europeans began exploiting the manpower of the Indian by taking advantage of the sedentary cultures.

The institution which became the basis for this exploitation was the *encomienda*, the large estate granted by the king of Spain. It was a form of the *señorío imperfecto* found in Andalucia, in which whole cities, towns, lands and their inhabitants were distributed among noblemen from northern Spain. Military orders also granted *encomiendas* to their members in foreign countries. In New Spain, the *encomienda* granted a Spaniard the "right" to payment and services in the form of work by a community or group of Indians. The basic idea was to take advantage of Indian labor power.

It was not possible to fit nomadic Indians into this mold, as their very mobility was their best defense, and so the *encomienda* system did not work in the northern provinces that now form part of the United States (except for New Mexico, where the sedentary society of the Pueblo Indians permitted its existence). Spanish policy in these areas was therefore to group around the missions those Indians who showed some tendency to be sedentary. Starting with these islands of colonization, the conquerors moved to consolidate their influence. They brought in the first cattle, horses, chickens, and pigs, and introduced instruments and techniques unknown to Indian agriculture, along with many new food products. The conquerors also brought new techniques to the mining and working of minerals; to textiles and a number of handicrafts; to political, juridical, and administrative institutions; and to language and culture in general.

Spanish colonialism introduced a social and economic

system that was basically feudal (although certain characteristics of early capitalism were also present). We find a sharp class division, with the white owners on one side and the great majority of the dispossessed on the other: Indians, mestizos, and mulattos. All three groups were held down by rapacious exploitation in the fields and the mines, on the cattle ranches, and in the newly formed cities. A process of cultural mixing took place that combined Indian patterns together with Spanish, Creole, and mestizo elements. The Chicano was born—a new breed of people, of a predominantly Indian and Spanish mixture.

In the northern provinces, a great lack of communication with the rest of New Spain and a natural isolation caused by geographic barriers, together with the small interest shown by the colonial powers in those frontier territories, produced a strong regionalism. Those in power let themselves be carried along by the weight of tradition, unaffected by changes in the outside world, while the working class lived in conditions of abysmal poverty with no hope of a different future. The master-peon division dominated everything. All institutions combined to maintain the existing state of affairs. The Church used its power to stupefy the Indians with the opiate of resignation and passivity, while carrying out economic exploitation through forced payments like the tithe.

Due to the isolation of these provinces, the revolutionary storm in Mexico which led to the war of independence from Spain did not waft even the faintest breeze of revolt to the north. Mexican power replaced that of Spain in 1821, and the same attitude of disinterest in the northern provinces was repeated. Life went on as in the past, except that in 1834 the lands and wealth of the Spanish missions in California were expropriated by the governor, creating a period of great prosperity for the private ranches and haciendas of that region.

The Conquered Provinces in 1848

At the time the Treaty of Guadalupe Hidalgo was signed, the territories newly taken from Mexico must have appeared to North American eyes just as they had appeared to the Spanish conquerors: full of promise, offering a chance to make fortunes quickly and with very little effort. But the mentality of the new "crusaders for civilization" was very different from that of the Spaniards, as was the economic, social, and political system it reflected. Burgeoning capitalism in the young republic had filled its citizens with limitless ambition. The arrival of the Anglo in the lost Mexican provinces brought a monetary economy complete with taxes, litigation over land ownership, mortgages, banking, and complex finance, all of which hit the native residents with bewildering force.

The imposition of capitalism came first to California and Texas, and more slowly to New Mexico. Only after the railroads reached New Mexico, opening new markets and thus creating a rise in land values, did the Anglo rapacity reach to full intensity. Swindling and stealing land became common practice, occurring with the support of local and federal authorities who did not hesitate to favor the right of the Anglo as conqueror over the just claims of the Mexican. According to Professor Clark S. Knowlton, between 1854 and 1930 the inhabitants of New Mexico lost a minimum of over 2 million acres belonging to private owners, 1.7 million acres of *ejidos* or common public lands, and 1.8 million acres of lands taken by the federal government without remuneration. This massive and still continuing loss of lands destroyed the economic basis of the rural Spanish-American towns, thus playing a crucial part in creating a huge disaster area marked by the high rate of poverty and social disorganization.[9]

But it was not the entire Spanish-speaking population that suffered severely from these actions in New Mexico. The old dominant class allied itself with the newcomers in common exploitation of the downtrodden. Later, as family and common land grants increasingly became the property of Anglos, a process of proletarianization began: a large number of New Mexicans began selling their labor to the mines and the railroads or as migrant agricultural workers.

If the process of conquest was somewhat gradual in New Mexico and not really consolidated until the early 1900s, it was sudden and violent in Texas and California. An avalanche of adventurers descended upon California with the discovery of gold, and under the new Anglo rule a license tax on "foreigners" was decreed in order to keep Mexican miners out of the picture—a historical irony that made people foreigners on their own lands. Shortly after this law was passed two thousand Anglo miners swarmed over the Mexican mining camp at the town of Sonora, shooting every Mexican in sight. They drove over a hundred into a corral and murdered or lynched dozens. As a result of the gringo riot, Mexicans abandoned the camp. This became the pattern all over southern California.

As in New Mexico, the dominant Hispano group joined the conquerors, placing their class interests above any fraternal feeling for those to whom they were bound by blood and cultural ties. History shows how easily the dominant classes adapt to new conquerors, and the conduct of the big Hispano landowners was no exception. But despite their efforts to ingratiate themselves with the new rulers, the Anglo intrusion was so overwhelming that by the end of the 1800s only a very few of the old aristocratic families retained a trace of their former wealth and power.

The Anglos, who generally thought only in terms of lynching, defrauding, and despoiling when they dealt with Mexicans, rapidly took over land by means of high taxes, arbitrary laws, and confirmation of deeds. The judicial structure was converted into a means of "legal" robbery, and we should remember that the judicial system operated in the

English language, which most Mexicans did not know. This combined with constant violence against the Mexicans to create the conditions for armed resistance. Fired with a spirit of revenge and a thirst for justice, Mexican miners and displaced property owners rose up. In California and Texas particularly, they organized for defense of their own. Then came the Anglo outcry: "Mexican bandits!" And this from those who had taken half a country by armed force!

With no way open to them except shameful submission or rebellion, the so-called bandits became the first to manifest protest by a colonized people. Juan Nepomuceno Cortina, who led a rebellion in Texas, charged in his manifesto of September 30, 1859, that his armed action was caused by the Anglo conspiracy to "persecute and rob us." He explained:

> There being no other crime on our part than that of being Mexican by birth . . . a secret conclave [has been formed] with the sole purpose of despoiling Mexicans of their lands to later reap the benefits of these for themselves. This is clearly proven by the conduct of Adolph Glavecke, who, invested with his rank of "sheriff," has spread terror among those not forewarned, making them believe that he will hang all Mexicans and will burn their ranches, in this way obliging them to leave the country. . . . Our conduct will give evidence to all the world that all Mexican aspirations are rolled into just one, that of continuing to be free men.[10]

Unfortunately, the rebellions which swept the Southwest did not occur at a favorable moment in history: the advance of U.S. capitalism was irresistible. Yet the image of these so-called bandits has remained engraved on the minds of those who saw in them an ideal of justice. Tiburcio Vásquez, executed by the Anglos in California in 1852, exclaimed before dying: "I fought many battles in defense of what I considered my rights and those of my compatriots. I believed that we were unjustly deprived of the social rights that should have been ours."

In Texas, the spirit of rebellion had always been strong, and it remained so. This province had first been invaded in the early 1800s by an adventurer believed to have been carrying out a mission for Thomas Jefferson. In 1820, an extensive land grant was made to a native of Connecticut, Moses Austin, who together with three hundred families played the Trojan Horse by setting up a base for Anglo subversion in Mexican Texas. Years before annexation, there was already definite interest in Texas lands:

> In every state of North America, there were numerous persons interested in land speculation. . . . Almost all of the Texas lands located between the Nueces and Sabina rivers to the south of Colorado had been acquired . . . by North American real estate companies or by individual speculators. North American capital, moreover, had assured itself of mining monopolies in many sections of Texas.[11]

After the war against Mexico, the contradictions between Anglos and Mexicans in Texas grew even sharper. Many Mexicans were thrown out of various Texas counties, forbidden to return, and required to travel on the public highways with special passes. In Goliad County, a resolution was passed stating the presence of the "greaser or Mexican peon" was an "intolerable indecency." Organized hunts, murders, robberies, and lynchings of Mexicans were everyday happenings, and cattle rustling and assaults on Mexican merchants were carried out with brutality and savagery: "The killing of Mexicans . . . is almost incredible. . . . Some [Texas] Rangers have degenerated into common man-killers. There is no penalty for killing, for no jury along the border would ever convict a white man for shooting a Mexican." [12]

The Role of Mexicans in the Economic Development of the Southwest

In addition to obscuring the history of violence against

Mexicans, Anglos try to hide the enormous importance of Mexican technology and labor in the economic development of the Southwest. The Mexican played a fundamental, decisive role in that development. The Mexican mining methods handed down from father to son provided the foundation for U.S. mining. Mexicans introduced the first system for extracting ore in dry-process mining, as well as the use of the pan for washing gold. They demonstrated the techniques for exploiting silver, copper, and quartz mines. And the majority of the mine workers themselves were of Mexican origin. As in almost all branches of labor, the Anglo worker received wages many times higher than those paid to the Mexican.

Mexican shepherds and shearers, with their deep knowledge and time-tested skills, gave the sheep-raising industry of the West its main impetus. Anglo owners kept the sheep hands in peonage, paying them starvation wages so that their debts passed from father to son and could never be paid. Cattle-raising had existed in the West for many years before the Anglo arrived. All the technology, terminology, utensils, and equipment for which the famous Anglo "cowboy" became known were taken from the Mexican *vaquero.* Saddle, bit, bridle, and spurs, the practice of bronco-busting, the skills of the lasso—all these and more are of Spanish and Mexican origin. The only original traits of the Anglo cowboy were his swaggering attitude and his predilection for killing Indians and Mexicans.

Knowledge of irrigation techniques was essential to developing the arid lands of the Southwest; these were assimilated from Indian and Spanish-Mexican experience, and the Anglos became prosperous farmers. It was also thanks to thousands and thousands of Mexican workers that all kinds of new plants and crops were developed. Mexican farmers sowed the cotton fields of Texas, Oklahoma, Arizona, and California, thus bringing a great increase in wealth to those regions. They planted and cultivated the many fruits, vegetables, and nuts that built huge Anglo wealth in California.

An equally important contribution was the development of the railroads. Since 1880, Mexicans have made up 70 percent of the section gangs on the principal railroads of the West; in 1930, the railroads employed more than 70,000 Mexicans, for the most part as common laborers. Mexican salaries were considerably less than those paid to whites for the same work on the Eastern and Midwestern railroad lines.

Agricultural and industrial development, mining, cattle-breeding, the wool industry, and the growth of communication were all made possible by the intensive use of Mexican know-how and labor. Many millions of dollars in profits were realized from the toil and technology of those same Mexicans who were murdered, reviled, humiliated, and mercilessly exploited, who lived in shocking conditions in unsanitary shacks at the edges of the fields, along the tracks, in the depths of mines, undergoing "schooling for a time in the meaning and methods of freedom."

Notes

1. Frederick Merk, *Manifest Destiny and Mission in American History* (New York: Knopf, 1963), pp. 24–25. Italics added.
2. Quoted in ibid., pp. 31–32.
3. Alonso Aguilar, *Pan-Americanism: From Monroe to the Present* (New York: Monthly Review Press, 1968).
4. A. Balenki, *La intervención extranjera en México, 1861–1867* (Mexico: Fondo de Cultura Popular, 1966).
5. Both quoted in Carey McWilliams, *North from Mexico* (1948; reprint ed., Westport, Conn.: Greenwood Press, 1968), p. 102. McWilliams is considered by many authors to be highly dedicated to the cause of ethnic and national minorities in the

United States. This book is outstanding for its scientific and literary value as well as for its sensibility and humanism, qualities which typify the committed scientist. For these reasons, and because the present book does not pretend to original historical research, we have referred frequently to this work.

6. Abiel Abbot Livermore, *The War with Mexico Revisited* (Boston: American Peace Society, 1850), pp. 248, 249.

7. Vicente Fuentes Díaz, *La intervención norteamericana en México (1847)* (Mexico, 1947).

8. The U.S. invasion of Mexican soil neither began nor ended with the war of 1846–1847. In 1836, General Gaines had occupied Nacogdaches, Texas, from July to December; in 1842, Commodore T. A. Jones had occupied Monterey, California. Then, in 1859, two hundred U.S. soldiers crossed into Mexico in pursuit of Juan Nepomuceno Cortina, a guerrilla fighting Yankee power in Texas. In 1866, General Sedgwick entered Matamoros to carry out a "police" operation and "protect North American citizens." In 1870, ships flying the U.S. flag went forty-five miles up a Mexican river on the pretext of pursuing a pirate ship; in 1873, U.S. troops repeatedly crossed the border at Remolina and Las Cuevas; in 1876, they again occupied Matamoros. In 1914 came the second bombardment and occupation of Veracruz, as well as numerous border penetrations. In 1916, there was the unsuccessful Punitive Expedition of General John Pershing in pursuit of Francisco "Pancho" Villa; in 1918, there were three recorded border crossings; there were six more in 1919. See Gastón García Cantú, *Las invasiones norteamericanas en México* (Mexico: Editorial ERA, 1971).

9. Clark S. Knowlton, *Among the Spanish-Americans.* Testimony presented at the Cabinet Committee Hearings on Mexican-American Affairs, El Paso, Texas, October 26–27, 1967.

10. Juan Nepomuceno Cortina, *Difficulties on the Southwestern Frontier*, Executive Document 52, December 30, 1859.

11. Ramiro Guerra y Sánchez, *La expansion territorial de los Etados Unidos* (Havana, 1962).

12. McWilliams, *North from Mexico*, p. 112, quoting George Marvin, *World's Work.*

2
The People

It is difficult to say exactly how many Mexicans were living in the territory taken over by the United States at the end of its war on Mexico. Some writers estimate the total at 75,000 to 84,000, of whom at least 60,000 were in New Mexico. But we must take into account the fact that these figures represent only those called "Mexicans," and exclude all Indians in the area. The different tribes of Pueblo Indians included many people who had lived with the Spaniards and mestizos for hundreds of years, identifying with them and sharing common blood relations, language, and religion. So the number of people who could be considered Mexicans should probably be raised by several thousand. (One cannot include the nomadic Indians—Apaches, Utes, Comanches, and others—who resisted colonization for many years. It was not until the 1880s that they were finally dominated and in many cases exterminated by the Anglo. While the Indian population of California was close to 100,000 in 1850, for example, by 1880 it had been reduced to about 20,000.)

The original Mexican population in the United States has been supplemented by people coming from Mexico who, over a period of time, have established themselves as U.S. citizens. Literature, history, and folklore all bear witness to this large movement of Mexicans across the border, long before it was controlled, measured, and classified. In one of the first migrations, miners from Sonora and other Mexican states went to California looking for gold. According to Leo Grebler, shepherds, *vaqueros*, and farmers crossed the border in both directions as though no boundaries existed.[1] For the inhabitants of northern Mexico, the conquered territories continued to form part of their own country. Treaties establishing borders between two nations, drawn up after an annexation war, are hardly enough to make natives of the lost lands conscious of a feeling of foreignness. For Mexicans of that era, their country continued to extend as far as it had for centuries.

In the late 1800s migration continued uninterrupted; control and estimates of the movement did not begin until the 1920s. One of the first studies of this migration was made by Dr. Manuel Gamio in 1926–1927 for the Social Science Research Council.[2] Dr. Gamio concluded that migration to the United States was basically an economic phenomenon— the logical result of an increased demand for workers in one country and a reserve of workers in the other. He established very precisely the main causes of northward migration: poor living conditions, low wages, unemployment, and the political instability of the times. He discovered that more than 70 percent of the migrants came from the Central Plateau region of Mexico, a zone where agricultural conditions were very difficult, the land was in the hands of a few large owners, and a great many *peones* were obliged to emigrate periodically (his description could very well fit the present reality of Mexico). If we combine these facts with the opening up of greater transportation links between the two countries and growing U.S. economic power, we can understand the essence of migration patterns.

Basically, the years from 1910 to 1929 were a period of massive immigration, while the years from 1930 to 1939 are called "the epoch of deportations." Immigration then boomed again after 1950 (see Table 1, Appendix). If we look at this pattern more closely, we find that the number of Mexicans coming to the United States rose sharply during the 1920s—with about one million in the year 1926 alone. This includes official immigrants, those who entered the country "illegally," and itinerant workers. That striking increase is directly related to the miserable economic conditions in Mexico after ten years of armed struggle. When the revolution there ended, many workers were back on the labor market and at the same time there was scant demand for labor. In the Southwestern United States, on the other hand, an extraordinary growth was taking place in agriculture, communications, and industry. Conditions both to the north and south of the border favored the immigration of Mexican workers into the United States.

Following this flourishing economic situation came the years of the Depression. Millions of unemployed Mexicans, Blacks, and Puerto Ricans faced intensified problems of survival in a racist country. For the Mexicans, the Anglo quickly found a "solution": the same attitude as that which had proclaimed "the only good Indian is a dead Indian" dictated that the best way to help the unemployed Mexicans was to get rid of them.

Legal and illegal immigrants, migratory workers, permanent residents, and even U.S. citizens of Mexican origin were thrown out of the country like common delinquents. A new method of compelling "voluntary departure" was found: the U.S. government simply suspended welfare payments and the people, driven by sheer hunger, left for Mexico. "Whereas during the 1920s we absorbed a population of 1 million Mexicans, in the 1930s we threw out about 500,000 people of Mexican origin," reported the President's Commission on Migratory Labor in 1951. What the Commission did not report was the experience of many who, having been born in the United States and knowing nothing of Mexico beyond what they had heard from their parents, were "expatriated" —regardless of the protections promised to U.S. citizens by

the Constitution and to Mexicans by the Treaty of Guadalupe Hidalgo.

During the period of the *"bracero* program" (1942–1947,
1951–1965) arranged between Mexico and the United States,
thousands of Mexicans set out for the U.S. as migrant
workers. Although the official agreement assured the *braceros* protection from exploitation and abuse, the Anglo
landowners soon found ways to get around this. The life of
the *braceros* and the misery they endured has been recorded
in detail by many official agencies as well as by historians.
While the *braceros* were considered legal immigrants, many
Mexican workers also came "illegally," that is, without
official papers. They were allowed to stay so long as the big
landowners and company directors needed them; when they
were no longer wanted, the U.S. government suddenly
appeared and deported them. These practices continue
today, and it has become clear that the U.S. Immigration
Service is a tool of the big economic interests. In 1953 alone,
875,000 Mexicans were picked up and expelled from the
United States; the following year the figure rose to over 1
million. These statistics reflect the dilemma faced by millions
of people living in that myth of prosperity and progress
called Mexico, where miserable living conditions force workers and farmers into the bitter adventure of emigration.

The Population Today

According to a March 1972 Census,[3] about 9.2 million
people in the United States identify themselves as being of
"Spanish" origin, including Mexicans, Puerto Ricans, Cu-
bans, and others. Of the 5.3 million of Mexican origin, about
85 percent live in the five Southwestern states of Arizona,
California, Colorado, New Mexico, and Texas. It is important to remember that these are government figures; Chicanos themselves believe their total number to be at least 10
million.

The population of Mexican origin has grown steadily (see Table 2, Appendix). According to official reports, the percentage of Chicanos in Texas has decreased and that in California has increased—a development that Dr. Gamio's study anticipated (see Table 3, Appendix). This is because the enterprises in California which have expanded rapidly are either those in which Mexicans traditionally have skills, or those which require large amounts of unskilled labor.

According to the 1970 Census, New Mexico has the highest proportion of Chicanos in any one state, with 407,286 people listed as of "Spanish language or Spanish surname" out of a total population of 1,015,998. The percentages in Arizona and Texas were 14 percent and 15 percent respectively. In the Southwest as a whole, based on the 1972 Census, Chicanos formed 12.3 percent of the total population (see Table 4, Appendix).

Close to 50 percent of the people of Mexican origin were under 18 years of age and the median age in March 1972 was 18.6 (see Table 5, Appendix). Contrary to what many people believe, the Mexican population in the United States does not live mostly in rural areas. In 1960, 79.1 percent of all Chicanos lived in cities. It is estimated that a third of all Chicanos lived in the metropolitan zones of sixteen cities, including Los Angeles (almost a million), San Antonio, El Paso, and Brownsville, Texas. In many Texas cities and even entire counties, people of Mexican origin form the great majority of the population.

We can see how the urban population has grown when we note that according to 1950 Census data, the number of Chicanos in cities was only 66.4 percent; in just ten years, the figure leaped almost 13 percent. In New Mexico, the rural population was reduced by 23 percent in the 1950s and in Colorado by 17 percent. The urbanization of Mexicans proceeds at a much faster rate than that of Anglos, Blacks, and others, and this process is most rapid in Texas and

California; 86 percent of the Chicanos in California lived in cities in 1960.

This urban increase seems to be closely related to the change that has taken place in the kinds of work Mexicans do. Many have been forced by circumstances to shift from their traditional occupation, agriculture, to service jobs and nonagricultural industry. The transition from rural to urban life has brought with it terrible social and human conflicts, for the change often takes place under pressure—when the people are faced with an urgent need to obtain work and better living conditions.

Notes

1. Leo Grebler, *Mexican Immigration to the United States: The Record and Its Implications*, Advance Report 2 (Los Angeles, Cal.: Mexican-American Study Project, 1966).
2. Manuel Gamio, *Mexican Immigration to the United States* (Chicaco: University of Chicago Press, 1930).
3. U.S., Bureau of the Census, *Current Population Report*, Series P-20, no. 238 (July 1972).

3
The Position of the Chicano Within U. S. Society Today

To understand the place that Mexicans occupy in U.S. society, we must consider a number of factors and isolate the most basic and important. U.S. government statistics are based on dividing people socially according to income, occupation, etc. This method does not conform with our view that social division in capitalist society arises from the existence of antagonistic social classes which are differentiated by the places they occupy in relation to ownership of the means of production: the fields, factories, mines and other sources of social wealth. Nevertheless, the information provided by official sources is of some use.[1]

Occupation and Income

The occupational *status* of the great majority of Chicanos is very low. They most often perform the kind of work called nonskilled or semiskilled. The 1960 Census showed that less than 20 percent of those of Mexican origin held jobs considered white collar or "nonmanual," while almost 50 percent of Anglos held such jobs. In a March 1972 Census report, 62.4 percent of the Mexican-origin men were blue-collar workers and only 17.5 percent were white-collar workers. The percentage of Mexican-origin workers doing white-collar

43

work remained about the same between 1960 (when it was 18 percent) and 1972.

Statistics show also that the number of Chicano agricultural workers and fieldhands has been cut down severely as agriculture has become more mechanized. (Of course, it should be remembered that many of these workers come from Mexico without legal documents and avoid being counted by the U.S. Census.) In industry, Chicanos are found working in textiles, furniture, glass, and ceramics—and being paid the lowest salaries. Few are employed in higher salaried industries, such as the manufacturing of chemical products.

Women of Mexican origin, along with Black and Puerto Rican women, dominate the field of service work, particularly domestic service (see Table 6, Appendix). Although 37.7 percent of these women performed white-collar work in 1969, this must be compared with the figure for Anglo women that year, 60.7 percent. The job situation for both Chicanos and Chicanas is in general very similar to that of Puerto Ricans and Blacks, except that a larger percentage of Chicanos work in agriculture than in service and domestic jobs, while for Blacks and Puerto Ricans the situation is the reverse.

The labor statistics suggest some general conclusions about the job situation:

1. The Chicano and those called "non-white" are always found in an inferior occupational status, the Anglo in a superior status.

2. The majority of Chicanos and "non-whites" perform jobs considered manual labor and so are more closely linked to production.

3. Chicanos and other "non-white" minorities are generally on the same occupational level, with a few small but not essential differences.

4. For the most part, Chicanos and other "non-whites" perform "semiskilled" and "unskilled" work while Anglos dominate the field of "skilled" labor.

5. Chicanos and other "non-whites" dominate the low status, domestic, and service jobs.

6. Workers fall into two well-defined groups: the Anglos on one side and the Mexicans and other "non-whites" on the other.

The effects that this unequal labor situation has on income (see Tables 7 and 8, Appendix) can easily be imagined. Although the *amount* of income has risen for Mexican families in the last ten or fifteen years, the *difference* between Chicano and Anglo incomes has not changed. In 1972, 39.5 percent of Mexican families in the United States were living on less than $6,000 while 75.7 percent of the non-Spanish-speaking families had an income of over $6,000. (This last percentage includes Blacks and other "non-whites," so the figure would be even higher for Anglos alone.)

The median income for families of Mexican origin in 1972 was $7,486; the median income for the total population that year was $10,285. The percentage of "low income" or poor Mexican-origin families that year was 28.9 percent as compared to 12.5 percent for the total population. This adverse relationship was worse for Chicanos in such states as New Mexico (41.5 percent poor families in 1960) and Texas (51.6 percent poor families in 1960). For "non-whites"—meaning mostly Blacks—in those states, about 58 percent of the families were below the poverty line. And within all these percentages, we find thousands of Mexican and Black families living on an annual income of less than $1,000. In 1969 there were 29,040 Mexican families living on less than $1,000 a year and 54,420 on less than $2,000.[2]

One of the constants of the capitalist system also appears in statistics: the inequality between men and women, even within the most exploited groups. In 1960, the average income for Mexican women workers in the Southwest was $1,202—less than half the income for men.

These statistics give us only an outline of the conditions in which minority groups live. The misery that exists in a country with such advanced technology, with one of the world's highest living standards, cannot be expressed in numbers. But what can be stated beyond any possible doubt is that this misery is the inseparable companion of Mexicans and Blacks.

Unemployment

A characteristic of the capitalist system is the permanent existence of what has come to be called a "labor reserve." Unemployment, the better-known name for this phenomenon, constitutes one of the many social ills found under capitalism. As can be expected, minority groups suffer from it to a greater extent than others. Thus we find that in 1960, Mexicans showed an unemployment rate of 8.5 percent compared to an Anglo rate of 4.5 percent (the "non-white" rate was 9.1 percent), and in 1972, 7.9 percent of the Chicanos were unemployed compared to the national unemployment rate of 6 percent. The percentage rises when we look at the youth alone: in 1972, 15.1 percent of Mexican males aged 16 to 24 were unemployed.

The lack of "skills" is an important factor in unemployment. It is logical to suppose that the more skilled the worker, the greater his chance of a job. Anglos, having more years of schooling, will necessarily have a higher employment rate than Mexicans and "non-whites." But this educational factor is by no means the fundamental cause of disparity in unemployment rates, as some authors would have us believe. This is a simplistic explanation, to which we will return.

Housing

Much has been written about the Black urban ghettos in the United States: the extreme deterioration of buildings; the high rate of infant mortality, disease, and crime; the desperation of the inhabitants. The same conditions exist in the Mexican barrios of the Southwest. In the 1960 Census, we find a variety of terms used to describe these conditions. One is "overpopulated"; 34 percent of Mexican families and 21 percent of "non-whites" lived in "overpopulated" homes in 1960, while only 7.7 percent of Anglo families lived in such dwellings. The category "ramshackle or run-down housing units" included 9 percent of all Mexican dwellings, 7.9 percent of non-white dwellings, and 1.3 percent of Anglo dwellings. On the basis of these figures, Mexicans are even worse off than "non-whites," which means that there is a very real basis for comparisons between the barrio and the ghetto.

The fact of segregation was demonstrated by the 1966 report of the Mexican-American Study Project, "Residential Segregation in the Urban Southwest," which analyzed the varying degrees of segregation between the Anglo majority and the Mexican and Black minorities. Taking 0 (zero) as representing the point where no segregation exists, and 100 as the point of absolute segregation (all groups in a particular location being concentrated in separate areas), the report evaluated segregation in thirty-five cities of the Southwest. The results are:

Anglos separated from both minorities	62.5
Anglos separated from Mexicans	54.5
Anglos separated from Blacks	80.1

While ratios varied from city to city, Blacks were more segregated than Mexicans in all places where the investigation was carried out. In Odessa, Texas, for example, the incidence of segregation for Mexicans was 75.5 and for Blacks 90.5. The highest rates of segregation for both groups was found in Texas: in Lubbock, it was 94.4 for Blacks. The lowest degree of segregation was found in Sacramento, California, with 30.2 for Mexicans.

Schooling and Illiteracy

The level of schooling of Mexicans in the five Southwestern states is extremely low. According to the 1960 Census, the median number of years of schooling for Mexicans in Texas was 4.7; in California, 8.6; in Colorado, 8.1; in New Mexico, 7.7; and in Arizona 7. Comparing these figures with those for other groups, we discover that "non-whites" had completed more years of school. In Texas, Colorado, and California the median number of years was 8.1, 11.2, and 10.5, respectively. The Anglo median was 11.6 years in the Southwest as a whole.

In 1963 Dr. David Martin carried out research in East Los Angeles—where the Mexican barrios are concentrated—and found that one out of every four people he interviewed had no formal education at all. They had never been to school. The fact that the Mexican level of schooling in Texas, Arizona, and New Mexico is lower than in other areas is due to the fact that the Mexican's economic and social situation in those states is by far the worst in the nation.

Herschel Manuel concluded that three factors combine to make it difficult for Mexicans to obtain an education and provoke the high drop-out rate among children of Mexican origin: the division of the community into two groups, Mexicans and Anglos, each lacking understanding of the other and with a certain degree of hostility toward each other; cultural differences; and language barriers.[3] He added that a large proportion of the Spanish-speaking children of the Southwest suffer the privations of low family income, and often of long-continued poverty. This last factor, which the author does not include as one of the essential "sources of difficulty," seems to us to be fundamental.

Discrimination

Discrimination against persons of Mexican origin has been a reality in the Southwest since the arrival of the first Anglos. We should not forget that the first people lynched in that area were Mexicans. In 1854, a killing a day was reported in Los Angeles, the majority of the victims being Mexicans and Indians. Américo Paredes has remarked on Anglo racism as it is reflected in popular novels:

> Nationalism becomes racism. The hero is always Anglo-Saxon, of course, and the cowards and "bad guys" are men with darker skin than his: Italians, Portuguese, Spaniards, Mexicans, or Indians. The plot shows us that the blond he-man is much more of a man than the "dark ones" and consequently is the one chosen by nature, according to the law of the jungle and the struggle for existence. This is nothing more or less than the figure of the superior man as the "blond beast," some forty years before Hitler.[4]

The encouragement of racism, year after year, through all the channels of communication, has endured to our day. During more than a century of white domination, the Mexicans and all other "non-white" groups have all had their share of physical violence, injustice, persecution, police brutality, the partiality of judges and juries made up of whites, cultural annihilation, and distortions of history. Racist declarations have punctuated official investigations of the situation of Mexicans in this country. For example: "The mass of the people in New Mexico are Mexicans, a hybrid race of Spanish and Indian origin, ignorant, degraded, demoralized, and priest-ridden."[5] During a series of meetings in California of the Lafayette Committee, which was investigating charges of police brutality in the suppression of a strike involving Mexicans, a county constable testified: "We protect our farmers here in Kern County. They are our best people; they keep the county going. But the Mexicans are trash. They have no standard of living. We herd them like pigs." [6]

Carey McWilliams recalls the "Zoot-Suit Riots" of 1943 in Los Angeles, when U.S. Marines, encouraged by a sensationalist press, organized a vicious and premeditated attack against Mexican youths. The police did not intervene to protect the youths at any point; only after the aggressors had disappeared did they put in an appearance:

> Four boys came out of a pool hall. They were wearing the zoot-suits that have become the symbol of a fighting flag. Police ordered them into arrest cars. One refused. He asked: "Why am I being arrested?" The police officer answered with three swift blows of the night-stick across the boy's head and he went down. As he sprawled, he was kicked in the face. Police had difficulty loading his body into the vehicle because he was one-legged and wore a wooden limb. Maybe the officer didn't know he was attacking a cripple.
>
> At the next corner a Mexican mother cried out, "Don't take my boy, he did nothing. He's only fifteen years old. Don't take him." She was struck across the jaw with a night-stick and almost dropped the two and a half year old baby that was clinging in her arms. . . . [7]

These events took place during the Second World War, when thousands of Mexicans were giving their lives in the battle against fascism and in defense of what was ironically called "the arsenal of democracy." "But that was in 1943," some would say, those whose desire to justify the U.S. system leads them to imagine that there has been substantial change in racist policies. In 1970, however, the U.S. Civil Rights Commission reported that this was not the case. Along with their report they sent a letter to the President, which said:

> We have found, through extensive field investigations . . . that there is widespread evidence that equal protection of the law in the administration of justice is being withheld from Mexican-Americans.

Our investigations reveal that Mexican-American citizens are subject to unduly harsh treatment by law enforcement officers, that they are often arrested on insufficient grounds, receive physical and verbal abuse, and penalties which are disproportionately severe. We have found them to be deprived of proper use of bail and of adequate representation by counsel. They are substantially underrepresented on grand and petit juries and excluded from full participation in law enforcement agencies, especially in supervisory positions.[8]

The Commission reported a multitude of cases of police violence against Chicanos which went unpunished and even uninvestigated. Such incidents are not isolated events but the expression of a sustained racist policy, tolerated by U.S. authorities.

The police, as well as Immigration and Naturalization agents and the guardians of the borders . . . have carried out periodical round-ups of Mexican-Americans or of anyone who "looks Mexican." There have been cases in which there has been gross negligence with respect to the safety of the lives and persons of those of Mexican nationality, as well as Mexican-Americans, negligence which has led to accidents and great loss of lives.[9]

Mass deportations and divestment of nationality, mentioned in the last chapter, are other examples of racist practices exercised against Mexicans. At midnight on June 17, 1954, one of the most sinister official campaigns against the Mexicans began, reminiscent of the methods and procedures of Nazi Germany. Thousands of agents raided the fields, factories, and barrios to hunt down and capture Mexican workers. A Los Angeles lawyer, Joseph Widoff, charged:

A condition exists here which is tantamount to martial law . . . it appears that all constitutional rights have been suspended in California and that homes are being entered without warrant of arrest, and papers and documents and

persons seized and arrested and driven out of the country
without any legal process or opportunity to exercise any legal
or constitutional rights, and that no person of Mexican
descent in California or surrounding area is safe and secure
. . . and that no person has any guarantees that he can obtain
a hearing under legal process to determine whether or not he
has any rights to remain in the United States. Never has such
action been taken before in peacetime. Only in war. . . .[10]

That was twenty years ago, but such practices have not
stopped. In 1973, the U.S. Immigration Service rounded up
thousands of Mexicans and once again threw them across the
border. People were taken out of their homes, picked up
while at work, grabbed at bus stops and off the street. If they
couldn't produce the right documents immediately, they
were on their way out of the country—and again, many were
in fact U.S. citizens.

If life for the Chicano is a constant struggle for survival
against unemployment, low salaries, disease, and misery, it is
also true that death comes quite easily to him in the racist
United States. An article in the Chicano movement newspaper *La Raza* reports on Chicano casualties in the war waged
by the U.S. government against the peoples of Indochina.
Data taken from Defense Department reports show that
persons with Spanish surnames in the Southwest represented
about 20 percent of all casualties in the armed services, and
23 percent in the Marine Corps alone. These percentages are
very high when compared to the official percentage of
Mexicans in the general population of the Southwest, which
was 12.3 percent in 1972. If we compare those percentages to
the number of men of military age, estimated at 13.8
percent, the disproportion becomes more specific and therefore even greater.

This information should not surprise us. The U.S. govern-
ment has always sent a great number of Blacks, Puerto
Ricans, Mexicans, and other "non-whites" to its battlefronts.
With the lure of bonuses and high salaries, with campaigns

exalting a world of "fun, travel, and adventure" and an atmosphere of fraternity, the government tries to get the cannon fodder needed for its wars of aggression. This was the case both in Korea and Indochina: enemies in the daily life of North American cities became brothers to kill and die in the forests and mountains for the U.S. empire.

Racism in the United States has deeply penetrated relations between workers. The ruling classes have for years set Mexicans against Blacks and Blacks against Puerto Ricans, using one group as scabs to break the strikes of another group, corrupting, blackmailing, jailing, deporting, murdering all of them to maintain their power. Every possible method has been used to divide the working class. Those in power have pampered and corrupted the white workers, instilling racism in them and pacifying them with higher salaries than those paid to Blacks, Mexicans, and so forth. The rulers have fomented selfishness and individualism, and hatred of those who threaten to take away hard-won jobs. In short, they have destroyed the class consciousness of the white worker. Dr. Gamio wrote in 1926 that Mexican labor is

a victim of the prejudices and an object of more or less hostility from the side of the American laborers themselves who naturally do not enjoy the competition of Mexican labor. As for the employers, it is evident that they sometimes take a part in disorganizing and destroying the attempts toward organization, of the Mexican laborers.[11]

And Carey McWilliams tells us:

With scarcely an exception, every strike in which Mexicans participated in the borderlands in the 'thirties was broken by the use of violence and was followed by deportations. In most of these strikes, Mexican workers stood alone, that is, they were not supported by organized labor, for their organizations, for the most part, were affiliated neither with the CIO nor the AFL.[12]

What is the basis for all this racism? We must answer that

question within a historical perspective, for racial prejudice
has existed for centuries. Its birth is closely linked with the
appearance of private property and subsequent wars of
conquest. Whenever the military, political, and economic
dominion of a people is in the hands of a foreign group, that
group tries to justify its rule. To the conqueror the new
vassals are inferior beings who must be watched, punished,
and killed if necessary.

From the contact between different peoples and races as a
result of conquest and exploitation, ethnocentrism emerged,
and from it, racial prejudice. For the Aztecs, who controlled
vast regions, the peoples they conquered were inferior—"chi-
chimecas," barbarians. Colonial powers—whether Portu-
guese, Spanish, French, or English—imagined that only their
language, their customs, their religion, even their vices and
crimes, were "civilized" and acceptable. For centuries, the
colonial powers assassinated, robbed, imprisoned, and sometimes exterminated the peoples of Asia, America, and Africa
on the altar of "Western civilization and Christianity." But
when the colonized peoples began to exercise their right of
rebellion, that which the white man had done in the name of
"law and order" became, when done by the "non-white,"
"vandalism, cruelty, the savagery of inferior beings."

On the American continent, the United States established
itself as the center of military and economic power after
England dropped to second place. U.S. imperialism, like
European colonialism before it, combined aggressive expansion with racism—which had already come of age among the
Anglos with their treatment of the native Americans and of
the Africans brought over as slaves. Each time the United
States invaded Mexico, Nicaragua, Cuba, Guatemala, Santo
Domingo, or Panama, the press, members of Congress, and
even "the man in the street" commented on the instability
and ignorance of those lazy people who must be helped to
resolve their affairs. The United States, as big brother and

guardian of the continent, must "protect" the peoples of Latin America from external and internal dangers.

The basis of this racist justification of U.S. expansionism is the economic interests of the dominant classes. Similarly, in order to exploit Blacks, Mexicans, Puerto Ricans, Asians, and others inside the country as cheap labor, these peoples must be made to seem inferior, humiliated, declassified, divided, their culture, history, and language wiped out. They must be made to believe that their misery is their own fault, because they lack the "enterprise" and "initiative" of the superior race. The ruling classes must convert these peoples to their own image, instilling material ambition and individualism in the exploited, thus preventing what the capitalist most fears: awareness of the true situation. Racism in the United States serves to cover up the true relationship between exploiters and exploited, between rich countries and poor countries. It serves to divert attention from the fundamental problem, the capitalist system.

Notes

1. In the sections that follow, we sometimes refer to 1960 statistics, sometimes to November 1969 statistics, and sometimes to March 1972 statistics. This is because different kinds of information were provided in different census reports. For example, the 1970 Census did not provide national statistics on persons of Mexican background; it used only a category called "Spanish heritage," and used this category only for certain kinds of information.
2. U.S., Bureau of the Census, *Current Population Report*, Series P-20, no. 213 (February 1971).
3. Herschel Manuel, *Spanish-Speaking Children of the Southwest: Their Education and the Public Welfare* (Austin, Tex.: University of Texas Press, 1965).

4. Américo Paredes, *Estados Unidos, Mexico y el machismo* (address read to the folklore division of the 37th Congress of Americanists, Mar de la Plata, Argentina, 1966).

5. *Badge of Infamy: Petition to the U.N.*, p. 10.

6. McWilliams, *North from Mexico*, p. 191.

7. Al Waxman, editor of *The Eastside Journal*, quoted in ibid., p. 249.

8. U.S., Commission on Civil Rights, *Mexican-Americans and the Administration of Justice in the Southwest* (Washington, D.C.: Government Printing Office, 1970), p. iii.

9. *Badge of Infamy: Petition to the U.N.*, p. 33.

10. Quoted in ibid., p. 34.

11. Gamio, *Mexican Immigration*, p. 134.

12. McWilliams, *North from Mexico*, p. 194.

4

The Chicano Movement

The Mexican minority lives in both a material prison of bad socioeconomic conditions and an ideological prison of prejudice, distortion, and confusion about what it considers to be its own reality. This confusion has been reflected in efforts to organize Chicanos, as well as in the mutual animosity which characterizes relations between the Mexican and Black populations—all of which has thus far prevented the unification of the two largest and most exploited groups in the Southwest.

Many Chicanos perceive their situation as due mainly to negative characteristics of members of their own community. During a visit to California, where I talked with and interviewed Chicanos at different economic levels, I frequently heard such remarks as: "If a person is bad off, it's because he wants to be. The whites are not to blame. It takes determination to get ahead." People of this mentality identified characteristics which they considered peculiar to Mexicans as a whole—"lack of tenacity," "not dedicated enough"—and admired those qualities spread by capitalist propaganda about the man who, on the basis of sheer willpower, manages "to get ahead in life."

A frequently heard opinion from university professors and students when asked about the causes of the difference in economic status between Mexicans and Anglos was that all problems arose from the Mexicans' lack of education. They believed that Mexican people in the United States are in poor circumstances because they lack an adequate education, without asking *why* their access to education has been blocked.

On the subject of the war in Indochina, many of those interviewed came out against the war for pacifist, political, or ideological reasons. One teacher in an adult school of mechanics expressed himself this way: "I am against the war and sending Chicanos to fight in it. Men are being lost who should fight the true battle—if they are going to die, let them die for La Causa, not for Vietnam." But others expressed support, as follows: "The country is in this war and we should support that decision. The United States must fulfill its agreement with the Vietnamese." A man living on a pension affirmed: "I was in Korea. If I could go again, I would. We should all fight. If the Communists aren't stopped, they advance." An eighteen-year-old woman student declared: "I wish there were no war, but I feel that men who don't want to go and fight are unworthy of this great nation." A metallurgic worker said: "I'm in favor of continuing the war, so the Communists won't keep on conquering places," and another person declared: "We have to stay until it's over. If we get out of there, they're going to say we're big cowards. We should hit them harder. Burning draft cards is about as low as you can get. Some Communist organization is behind that." A housewife who opposed using Mexicans in the war gave the following reason: "We have wars right here, with all these restless Negroes thirsting for revenge. We don't have to look anywhere else for trouble."

It seemed that as a result of the Anglos' rejection of the Mexican people, they tried to seem more "patriotic" than the Anglos themselves, reaffirming their "patriotism" by defending the foreign and domestic policies of the U.S.

government. Yet this psychological mechanism is a minor factor in explaining the existence of attitudes better suited to a general in the Pentagon than to a humiliated and exploited Mexican. There must be other reasons.

During that same visit I investigated the opinions of Mexicans living in the Watts district of Los Angeles in studies done by the University of California sociology department shortly after the rebellion of August 1965. Racial prejudice, although it did not reach the same degree as that shown by the Anglos, was expressed in a feeling of superiority toward the Black population and a certain suspicion or distrust about the explosions of violence in the Black community. I heard statements of this nature: "I have never believed that the Negroes could be compared to Mexican-Americans because we respect and love our country, the United States. The Negroes, on the other hand, still have in their veins the blood of savages. When their savagery comes over them, they do not care who they kill." Most Mexicans declared themselves against the Black rebellion and in sympathy with, or even in favor of, the brutal way that the authorities "put down the riot." At the same time, many were conscious of the importance of unifying the Mexican people with the Blacks in a common defense against the exploitation they both suffer; they did, however, emphasize their rejection of violent methods.

Some authors have attempted to explain the Mexicans' racist attitudes toward Blacks by pointing out the acute competition for jobs, apartments, government grants, scholarships, etc. But this is a situation created by the ruling classes and used deliberately to "divide and conquer." A more basic reason is the fact that the Mexican population in the United States has been subjected to a long process of ideological conversion, of having their attitudes molded by a capitalist system. They have been deliberately infected with all the values—including racism—of the dominant society.

Those Mexicans who try to seem more "patriotic" than the Anglos themselves are one example of the ideological molding process.

All channels of information, teaching, and education are at the service of the dominant class in the United States, for the purpose of alienating public consciousness in the interests of this class. The Cuban edition of *The Invisible Government* by David Wise and Thomas B. Ross, quotes a statement by John Swinton, former editor-in-chief of the *New York Times*, in which he identifies this process as he perceived it:

> Our much boasted freedom of the press means freedom of the rich to possess and to impose upon public opinion the world as they see it, through the eyes of great wealth. No law deprives the United States of its freedom, there is no need to . . . the news items we receive are mutilated, distorted and twisted in favor of the rich, and against the poor. We are the instruments and vassals of the rich who act behind the scenes. . . . Our talent, our possibilities and our life, everything belongs to others. We are intellectual prostitutes.

Such confessions reveal one small aspect of the intensive and constant campaign which the dominant classes of the United States carry on to quiet the consciences of its citizens and produce fascist mentalities. An example of the results is found in the following excerpt from a questionnaire circulated in 1965 after the Watts conflict:

Q. What kind of people were against [the rebellion]?

A. The greatest part of the population, including some Negroes. To sum up: the good people.

Q. What kind of people supported [the rebellion]?

A. Communistic Negroes.

Q. Do you believe that the authorities acted right or wrong?

A. Wrong.

Q. Why do you think that?

A. Because they should have killed all of them.

Since then, the Chicanos, who are mostly young people, are avidly learning about what is really taking place in the country and about the role that the United States plays in the world. Frobén Lozada, then head of the Latin American Studies department at Merritt College in California, said in a November 1969 interview:

> How can this .016 percent of the total population [the ruling class in the United States] run the country? They have several tricks. One of them is racism. Divide and rule is the name of the game. . . . Another trick that the ruling class uses is to always make the victim look like a criminal. . . . Zapata, Pancho Villa, are made to look, in our eyes, as if they were criminals, and they keep pulling that trick on us. It's brought up to date. . . . The people in Washington and elsewhere point the finger of accusation and say, "Fidel is trying to export revolution." In the meantime, this country continues to export *counterrevolution*. So they turn the tables on everything in order to continue to deceive the people.[1]

Propaganda aimed at forcing the oppressed to defend his oppressor continues to claim its victims among Mexicans, but many visible changes have taken place in the realm of political consciousness. From California to Texas and all across the country, Chicanos are engaged in the battle against what Rafael Guzmán calls "cultural imperialism." We should remember that Mexicans in the United States not only are subject to ideological manipulation but also have been the victims of an attempt to rob them of their culture, language, and traditional forms of human relations. The oppressor has tried to uproot their origins, deform their history or ignore it, and inculcate the conqueror's point of view. The battle against this whole panorama of cultural imperialism has been a major characteristic of today's Chicano movement.

We see today's movement as the fourth period of political struggle by Mexicans in the United States. The first began at the very moment when the Anglos conquered the Southwest, the period of guerrilla activity led by the "bandits" mentioned in Chapter 1, who represented the reaction to conquest: they responded to the conqueror's violence with violence by the people. Without exception, these early movements were violently repressed, their leaders imprisoned, murdered, or driven into exile, and they resulted in increased distrust, hatred, and resentment, and very little political activity by Mexicans for some fifty years.

The second period began in the 1920s with the emergence of organizations which reflected the integrationist aspirations of the middle strata of the Chicano population. These organizations represented the first attempt by the middle strata to change the existing way of cutting up that cake called "the American way of life." The Order of the Sons of America, founded in San Antonio in 1921, accepted as members only "United States citizens" and its main goal was to show the Anglos that the "Sons of America" were very different from "those other Mexicans who only cause problems." They made repeated and unsolicited declarations of loyalty to the United States. The League of United Latin American Citizens (LULAC) also sought integration into the system. A few years after the U.S. bombardment of Veracruz and the bloody U.S. expedition in search of "Pancho" Villa, they declared that their goal was "to develop within the members of our race the best, purest, and most perfect type of a true and loyal citizen of the United States of America." [2]

During these same years, the 1920s and 1930s, when middle-strata or petit-bourgeois Mexicans were trying to enter the system by the back door, thousands of Mexican workers were waging a strong labor fight. All over California, Arizona, Texas, New Mexico, and other states they went on strike for better wages and living conditions as well as an end to racist employment practices. The answer of the dominant classes to their demands was the deportation, jailing, or murder of Mexican labor leaders and a wave of violent repression against farmworkers, miners, and others—including their families.

The third period began after the Second World War, which brought a change in both the objective and subjective conditions of the many thousands of Mexicans who took part in it. The fact of having fought for the United States fixed in the minds of those who survived the idea that it was their inalienable right to demand a better life in that country. The war and postwar years also saw an increase in Mexican migration to the cities and a relative increase in the number of middle-class Mexicans as a result of the demand for labor and increased prosperity during those years.

The organizations formed at that time, many of which still exist, aimed at solving concrete social, economic, and political problems through the channels offered by U.S. society. This meant working within the system, using the tricks and various kinds of pressure peculiar to that system with the goal of winning greater concessions from Anglo power—but without casting doubt on the legitimacy of the institutions born from that power. Activity centered around getting Mexican representation in government institutions. Although these organizations included many with a sincere concern for the living conditions of poor Chicanos, they were oriented mainly toward the limited aspirations of the middle strata—although in a less obvious way and with a more aggressive style. They took the usual forms of social and political climbing, opportunism, and a paternalism that assigned no importance to organizing the masses.

Out of these groups, together with Mexican businessmen, landlords, and others closely allied with Anglo power, came a series of professional politicians. These are the individuals whom Chicanos jokingly call "Cocos" (for coconuts, brown on the outside and white inside). With few exceptions, the Cocos have been nothing more than token Mexicans, used to demonstrate the increasing "democratization" of U.S. society. These so-called leaders never miss an opportunity to call for the integration of Mexicans into a society that despises and exploits them, and they have been quick to denounce or subvert militant Chicanos. It was Senator Henry B. Gonzalez of Texas who in April 1969 accused a Chicano youth organization in that state of receiving assignments and help from Cuba. (Exactly the same accusations were made six months later by Anglo government officials against a nationalist youth organization in the revolutionary movement of French-speaking people in Quebec. It seems that those in power must always attribute to "outside agitators" actions which are provoked by economic and social causes.) The existence of such Cocos as Senator Gonzalez and Senator Joseph Montoya of New Mexico confuses some Chicanos, who judge their progress by the number of Spanish surnames in high office. The aware Chicano understands very well that under present conditions, even if a Henry B. Gonzalez were in the White House it would not make life better for the Chicano people as a whole.

The Chicano movement today, the fourth period of activity, is heir to the combative spirit of the nineteenth-century patriots and the popular strike movement of the 1930s, and represents the continuing resistance of a colonized people. It began in the 1960s, under the stimulus of the Black movement for civil rights and the general atmosphere of social protest in the United States. The war in Vietnam, the sharpening of racial and social conflicts in general, the rising cost of living, the increase in repression and right-wing activity, all helped to create a new awareness. Moreover, continuing migration to the cities made it possible to do certain kinds of organizing that had not existed before. Finally, the number of young Chicanos had increased, producing a group that could help create a new ideology for the Chicano people.

That ideology, which some writers call *Chicanismo*, projects a new image of the Mexican—both for himself and for the Anglo. Like Black nationalism, Chicano nationalism builds up pride in one's ethnic and cultural origins. It awakens the feeling of unity and fraternity among La Raza—words that literally mean "the race" but specifically represent the Chicano people with their common origins and experience. The national identity of the Mexican people, of La Raza or the Chicanos, has surged forth. The Chicanos are affirming pride in their true history and rejecting the dominant society's values and ideology. "*Chicano* ideologies . . . reject what they call the myth of American individualism. . . . If Mexicans are to confront the problems of their group realistically they must begin to act along collective lines." [3] In other words, they must unite as a people, with pride in their peoplehood—not on the basis of class, age group, or geographic area, but on the basis of their unique, shared experience as a people.

Inspired by these ideas of cultural nationalism, many young Chicanos have launched a wave of artistic activity— poetry, painting, sculpture, theater work, dance, novels, and so forth—as well as programs for the study of Chicano history. Students have struggled to get educational programs oriented to, and directed by, Chicanos themselves. They have also set up their own schools, after much effort and Anglo opposition, such as the Jacinto Treviño College in Texas and the Tlatelolco School started by the Crusade for Justice in Denver. These schools aim to educate Mexican students and future teachers to the reality and true needs of their people.

Chicanos are trying to restore their group identity and remain united in the face of attacks or subversion by the system. They are building on the ideas of liberty and independence of such Mexican revolutionary leaders as Emiliano Zapata and Francisco Villa, and the symbols of our mythical Indian past. Looking at the ideas of José Vasconcelos on the "Bronze Race," they are divesting those ideas of their inherent racism and taking them as a means of expressing solidarity with the peoples of Latin America who have the same masters and the same enemy. They are striving to define themselves in terms that will distinguish them from the Mexican of past and present, dominated by the gabacho or gringo; questioning and doubting and learning, at the crossroads of an uncertain destiny but with the certainty that the future will be better for the inhabitants and true owners of the Southwest.

To the Chicano, the Southwest is Aztlán, the mythical name of the Aztec Indians' homeland somewhere in northern Mexico, which they left when they set out on their long migration to what is today Mexico City. El Plan Espiritual de Aztlán, adopted in March 1969 at the first national Chicano Youth Conference in Denver, Colorado, states:

> In the spirit of a new people that is conscious not only of its proud historical heritage, but also of the brutal "gringo" invasion of our territories, we, the Chicano inhabitants and civilizers of the northern land of Aztlán, from whence came our grandfathers, reclaiming the land of their birth, and consecrating the determination of our people of the sun, declare that the call of our blood is our power, and our inevitable destiny. . . . Aztlán belongs to those that plant the seeds, water the fields, and gather the crops, and not to the foreign Europeans. We do not recognize capricious frontiers on the bronze continent. Brotherhood unites us, and love for our brothers makes us a people whose time has come and who struggle against the foreigner gabacho who exploits our riches and destroys our culture. With our heart in our hands and our hands in the soil, we declare the independence of our mestizo nation. We are a bronze people with a bronze culture. Before the world, before all of North America, before all our brothers in the bronze continent, we are a nation, we are a union of free pueblos, we are AZTLÁN.

Because of the emphasis on unity based upon nationality, many different currents flow into and make up the Chicano movement, all expressed in different ways. It could be said that the main characteristics of the Chicano movement have been heterogeneity and localism. For example, the tactics and organizing methods of the farmworkers' movement led by César Chávez have been very different from those used by Reies López Tijerina of the land grant movement or Rodolfo "Corky" Gonzales of the Crusade for Justice. Those three groups are in turn different from the movements led by students and university intellectuals. But one characteristic unites all the organizations: for the first time in years, Mexicans are expressing themselves politically in a way that is independent of Anglo tutelage.

The present movement does not beg for favors under the guidance of some powerful figures in the U.S. Congress. Leaders like "Corky" Gonzales and César Chávez have fought to see that the masses participate in and support any major political activity. Thousands of Mexicans have mobilized to go on strike, to walk out of schools in protest against the educational system, to protest U.S. occupation of their lands, to fight the welfare system, to resist the war in Vietnam and the draft, to protest prison conditions, to support and raise funds for the entire struggle. Newspapers and magazines have sprung up in many Chicano communities to express the new spirit of identity and protest; some examples are *La Raza, Basta Ya!* (Enough!), *El Gallo* (The Rooster), *La Gente* (The People), and *El Grito del Norte* (The Outcry of the North).

This movement coexists with the traditional forms of struggle by more conservative Chicano groups. Relations between the two are at times mutually helpful, at other times more or less antagonistic, and at times in open and irreconcilable contradiction. Attempts are often made to coopt or buy off the radical groups, and "liberal" white forces have tried to keep Chicano organizations from becoming truly radical. The Kennedys, particularly Robert Kennedy, worked hard to win Chicano support—especially when elections were coming up. Various church groups also have tried to keep movement organizations under their ideological control.

But despite all these efforts by the opposition, many Chicanos have begun to understand that their struggle is not merely a case of winning a strike or eliminating discrimination. Many realize that they are united with Latin America for reasons other than their common racial and historical background. They realize that things are bad not because of the bad faith of a few people, nor because they lack formal education, but because there is a system that exploits Mexicans, Blacks, and whites; that hides the reality of brotherhood and alienates people to such a degree that they disown their own class and race. From this recognition has come such statements as the following, by Frobén Lozada:

We look at the barrio . . . not as something confined by arbitrary city limits determined by corrupt politicians who want you to think in no broader terms than your own barrio so that you won't bother to think of the people of the Third World as brothers. We look at our barrio as one not restricted or confined to arbitrary city limits. Our barrio goes beyond these fictitious city limits and extends into the Plaza de las Tres Culturas in Mexico City. Our barrio is projected into the favelas in Brazil. Our barrio extends into the jungles of Bolivia and the jungles of Vietnam. And that's what our barrio is! Our barrio, in fact, is the whole world, wherever the oppressed might be.[4]

The more this kind of awareness grows, the more repression grows. While police brutality against Chicanos is nothing new, it has increased in the last few years. At the same time, a killing or beating that might once have gone almost unnoticed now produces marches, picket lines, and other protests.

Some of the worst brutality has occurred in Los Angeles, California. On August 29, 1970, three Chicanos were killed shortly after an antiwar demonstration by some 10,000 of La Raza. With tear gas and clubs, police attacked the demonstrators who had gathered in a park to hear music and speeches. The community rose up in protest against the police actions; that same afternoon, police killed noted journalist Rubén Salazar, Angel Díaz, and a Chicano youth named Lyn Ward. Hundreds were wounded. Five months later, on January 31, Los Angeles police attacked another Chicano demonstration and left another man dead.

Police repression also includes imprisonment: Reies López Tijerina was locked up for over two years not because of any crime he had committed but because he had defended and represented Chicanos robbed of their lands in New Mexico.

Certainly one of the greatest fears of the ruling classes in the United States is the possibility that the most exploited groups will join forces against them. Therefore, when César Chávez began the famous grape strike in Delano, California, in 1965, bringing together Mexican and Filipino farmworkers, not only the bosses but also the U.S. government moved to stop them. When a national and international call went out for people to boycott grapes, the U.S. Defense Department began buying them up in huge quantities to support the growers. In spite of such efforts the strike movement grew and with it the unionization of many workers. Chávez' United Farm Workers have won a series of victories and spread their activities to many states.

"Now, more than ever," Chávez has observed, "we are convinced that our American ideal of equality will only be an empty dream until all the poor are organized in strong unions that are responsible to their members." The farmworkers' Plan de Delano says: "Because we have suffered—and we are not afraid to suffer—in order to survive, we are ready to give up everything, even our lives, in our fight for social justice. We shall do it without violence, because that is our destiny." [5]

In 1973, the United Farm Workers found itself once again fighting for its very life. The grape contracts, won after a long struggle, expired in that year. The Teamsters union moved in to take them over, with the help of the growers, using every method from trickery to violence. The small farmworkers' union once again had to put up an agonizing struggle against the rich powerful bureaucrats of the Teamsters, agriculture, and government.

Chicanos have also used electoral methods to gain control over their communities, but in a new form. Unlike the Cocos, they have denounced both the Republicans and the Democrats and organized their own party, La Raza Unida Party, which has spread from coast to coast. In towns and cities where Chicanos form a large majority of the population, its candidates have won key local offices; the best-known is Crystal City, Texas, where La Raza Unida won control of the school board and the city council. Crystal City is located in the Rio Grande Valley, where the Texas Rangers have long had a free hand to arrest, beat, or kill Mexicans at will; today they are not allowed to enter Crystal.

In view of the success of the party and the enthusiasm it has created, La Raza Unida leaders are trying to continue building the party on a broader basis and with grander objectives. José Angel Gutiérrez, founder of the party in Texas and a leader of MAYO (Mexican American Youth Organization) expressed the goal in a speech in San Antonio on May 4, 1970:

> In 1960 there were twenty-six Texas counties in which Chicanos were a majority, yet not one of those counties was in the control of Chicanos. If you want to stand there and take that, you can. You can be perfectly content just like your father and your grandfather were, con el sombrero en el mano [with hat in hand]. . . .
>
> We are the consumers, we are the majority. We can stop anything and we can make anything in south Texas if we stick together and begin using common sense. This third party is a very viable kind of alternative. It's a solution. For once you can sit in your own courthouse and you don't have to talk about community control because you are the community.

La Raza Unida leaders recognize the usefulness of electoral legality in propagating Chicanismo among the masses of

Chicanos. They recognize that the party is a powerful tool for educating Chicanos about political, economic, and social issues. The battle for electoral representation is a tool that can be used, in an aggressive way, to organize.

Rodolfo "Corky" Gonzales emphasizes the role of new party as an educational tool. Founder and director of the Denver community organization, the Crusade for Justice, "Corky" is known for his dedication to serving the people and for his poems (especially "I Am Joaquín"), and other writings. One of the most enthusiastic supporters of Chicano nationalism and self-determination, he has said:

If you try to climb up a stairway, you have to start with the first step. You can't jump from the bottom of this floor to the top of those bleachers . . . so you start using those tools that are necessary to get from the bottom to the top. One of these tools is nationalism . . . which means that we have to be able to identify with our past and understand our past, in order that we can dedicate ourselves to the future, dedicate ourselves to change.

We have to start to consider ourselves as a nation. . . . We can understand that we are a nation of Aztlán. We can understand and identify with Puerto Rican liberation. We can understand and identify with black liberation. We can understand and identify with white liberation from this oppressing system once we organize around ourselves.

We have to understand that liberation comes from self-determination, and to start to use the tools of nationalism to win over our barrio brothers . . . who are still believing that machismo means getting a gun and going to kill a communist in Vietnam because they've been jived about the fact that they will be accepted as long as they go get themselves killed for the gringo captain. . . . We have to win these brothers over, and we have to do it by action. . . . You have to understand that we can take over the institutions within our community. We have to create the community of the Mexicano here in order to have any type of power.[6]

The Chicano student movement contains all of the ideological tendencies already mentioned. Many students have put themselves at the service of the mass movements, particularly that of the farmworkers. Others have stayed within the framework of the student struggle, while supporting their people as a whole in certain ways. There also exist some who clearly represent middle-class interests and who maintain an escapist, superficial attitude in the face of their people's problems.

Another aspect of the academic field of struggle has been the strong criticism of sociological studies from an Anglo viewpoint. In April 1967 Nick Vaca initiated this criticism with his "Message to the People," joined the next year by Octavio I. Romano's articles in the Berkeley, California, journal *El Grito*. Both attacked the studies by U.S. anthropologists, sociologists, historians, and psychologists which are filled with racism, paternalism, stereotypes, psychological generalizations, ethnocentric evaluations, and cultural cliches, and which are based on questionable investigative methods. To these "intellectual mercenaries of our time," as the first editorial in *El Grito* called them, "Mexican-Americans are simpleminded but lovable and colorful children who, because of their rustic naivete, limited mentality and inferior, backward 'traditional culture,' choose poverty and isolation instead of assimilating into the American mainstream and accepting its material riches and superior culture." [7]

Chicano intellectuals understand the function of these stereotypes in a society where the causes of economic exploitation, racism, and misery must be explained outside the system from which they originate, and in the cultural or psychological characteristics of the oppressed groups. This society rents, buys, or produces its intellectuals and assigns them the task of putting the blame for social evils on the victims of those evils! Thus emerge the "experts," the "specialists," who with academic smugness and complicated terminology, try to cover up or justify the truth about social relations under capitalist exploitation.

Dr. Romano urges that the concept of "historical culture" replace the concept of "traditional culture," which, besides being vague and ambiguous, imposes a static and nonhistoric vision on reality. In using it, the anthropologists and sociologists have taken a series of characteristics which should be defined in the context of concrete and historical conditions and extended them to *all* Mexicans, classifying Chicanos once and for all time. Instead of shedding light on the real situation of the Chicano people, these studies support the racist ideas and cultural stereotypes that are so popular among many Anglos—all in the name of so-called "social science."

This has been a brief glimpse of the Chicano movement, a movement of great variety, with a common base in a consciousness of exploitation and oppression together with a search for a way to liberation. The process of a people becoming aware and radicalized, of consciousness-growing, is one that evolves day by day; it is surprising what changes can take place in a very short time. The Chicano movement itself will find the best way to organize and unify the most determined, dedicated elements among the Mexican people.

In the past year there has also been a rising consciousness in the Chicano movement of class questions. This consciousness had been intensified by Chicanos seeing the results of U.S. efforts to passify, coopt, and divide the movement with government favors and well-paying jobs given to a few select Chicanos—while the masses continue to live in the same conditions as before. In other words, the U.S. system tries to build up the tiny Chicano middle class and tie it tightly to the capitalist structure with chains of self-interest. This has the effect of making the class turn its back on poor Mexicanos and reject any real revolutionary change. Clearly, there is no liberation when a few persons are better off but the people as a whole still suffer.

"Corky" Gonzales spoke out strongly about this problem in an October 1972 speech prepared for the Congress on Land and Cultural Reform in Albuquerque, New Mexico. He condemned "the *políticos*, professionals, and businessmen of our group who sell their dignity . . . to the highest bidder." As "Corky" said, the cultural step of achieving Chicano identity has been taken. The second step of using nationalism as a tool to organize is being taken. The third step is understanding the class system and how it is used to divide Chicanos. Mexicanos must not have in their own group a copy or duplicate of the class system of the oppressor society. As "Corky" said, "The Chicano struggle . . . must embrace a collective struggle of the people against individual selfishness, greed, and opportunism . . . The masses of our people are in need and it is they who suffer, and it is for them and ourselves that we must educate, elevate, liberate."

Notes

1. Frobén Lozada, "Why Chicano Studies?" in *La Raza!* (New York: Pathfinder Press, 1970), pp. 13–14.
2. LULAC Constitution, 1929, Article 2, quoted in Joan Moore and Alfredo Cuélla, *Mexican Americans* (Englewood Cliffs, N.J.: Prentice-Hall, 1970), p. 143.
3. Ibid., p. 153.
4. Lozada, "Why Chicano Studies?", p. 15.
5. "Plan de Delano," in *Basta!* (Delano, Cal.: Farm Worker Press, 1966).
6. Chicano Liberation Symposium, California State College, Hayward, California, November 13–14, 1969.
7. *El Grito, A Journal of Contemporary Mexican-American Thought*, no. 1 (Fall 1968), editorial.

5
Analysis and Conclusions

Many writers have portrayed the Mexicans in the United States as a linguistic, racial, or cultural minority, or simply a minority, concepts based on isolated factors that do not characterize all Mexican-Americans. Few researchers have gone very deeply into the basic question: What *kind* of minority are the Mexicans in the United States?

Dr. Manuel Gamio brought the problem into correct focus when he stated that the Mexican element constitutes a unique nationality in the United States. Carey McWilliams concludes:

> Unlike most European minorities in America, Mexicans have been rooted in space—in a particular region—over a long period of years. One of the important factors . . . has always been their relation to, and their feeling about the region in which they are concentrated . . . they are more like the typical minority in Europe than like the typical European minority in the United States. Mexicans were *annexed by conquest*, along with the territory they occupied and, in effect, their cultural autonomy was guaranteed by a treaty.[1]

There are few countries today that do not have minority groups with populations whose cultural, racial, linguistic, and other characteristics differentiate them from the majority.

Many could be called multinational; they contain various "ethnic groups." But what the specialist calls an "ethnic group" is really *a people*.

The development of political consciousness in an ethnic group signifies the existence of a nationality, so long as that group does not have political power. Once power is attained, this nationality is transformed into a nation. But the development of political consciousness is a subjective factor; it alone cannot give a precise idea of how a nation comes into being.

Joseph Stalin described a series of events that could be observed in the developing of nations. In the first place, he said that the process takes place at a specific moment in history, the stage of rising capitalism, when the bourgeoisie consolidates itself as the force capable of transforming a feudal structure and laying the economic and social foundations for the emergence of a nation. He described a nation as a "historically evolved, stable community of language, territory, economic life, and psychological make-up manifested in a community of culture." [2] Those people who had all these attributes, but still could not become independent states, were integrated under the domination of the most powerful nations and thereby became national minorities or minority nationalities.

Among the various historical events that have served to create multinational states are conquest, war, voluntary migration, or migration forced by economic need. "It is capitalism which drives them into other regions and cities in search of a livelihood. But when they enter foreign national territories and there form minorities, these groups are made to suffer by the local national majorities in the way of limitations of their language, schools, etc." [3]

In the case of Mexican-Americans both conquest and economic need are principal elements in the formation of a people or a nationality—the Chicano National Minority—composed of the original inhabitants of the conquered territory, and those who emigrated from Mexico. This second group has maintained its ties with the nation of its origin, and has been an important factor in preserving cultural traditions and keeping alive the consciousness of national origin. But it is not possible to define the Mexican minority racially, since the people do not constitute a specific race with certain broad characteristics in common. As a result of a long process of mixing, the Mexicans do not have racial homogeneity; the Mexican is a mestizo. We find everything from Caucasoid to Mongoloid and Negroid physical types among Chicanos. The Chicano is not exploited and discriminated against solely because of the color of his skin, his language, or his culture, but because of a whole series of characteristics that enter into the concept of nationality.

The Mexicans in the United States differ from other minorities because of their history, because they inhabit an area which they once considered to be their own, and because of the persistence with which they have preserved their language, group spirit, and certain cultural traditions. What they suffer in common with other minorities is economic exploitation, racism, and the same miserable living conditions. Thus the significant feature of the Chicano minority is its national origin; they make up a national minority, although this concept must be understood within the framework of the special historical characteristics of the Southwest.

Different Approaches to the Question of the Chicano National Minority

As we mentioned before, many who have studied what they call "the Mexican problem" tend to believe that the most important cause is lack of education and skills, and that the problem will be solved when teaching methods are perfected to "understand the Mexican child" and when new generations have more opportunity for education. Others place great importance on certain aspects of the culture: some publications, for example, emphasize "the language problem" and see in the Spanish language both the curse and the salvation of Mexicans. Still others maintain that the cultural contrast between Mexican and Anglo society is so strong that the Mexican takes refuge in his own group, in the traditional pattern that he grew up with. A psychological expression of "the problem" springs from this approach, such as the Mexican "prefers to rest in the security of his native world." This current of thought insists both on the "cultural clash" and attendant psychological traumas and on the language problem. Very few writers have discussed the problem from a broader frame of reference—within the perspective of the capitalist system, taking into account the fact that Chicanos constitute a national minority hemmed into a specific socioeconomic structure at a particular moment in history.

From the moment when the Anglos took possession of the lands of the Southwest, Mexican people became part of the new United States society as an exploited group, first because their new rulers robbed them of certain means of production (such as the land and cattle), and second because they came from an economically less-developed society, and thus were at a disadvantage in the technological society of the United States. The Mexican has been exploited both because he forms part of a conquered minority and because he belongs to the great majority of the dispossessed.

Above all it is important to remember that Mexicans are a "conquered" people in the Southwest, a people whose culture has been under incessant attack for many years and whose character and achievements, as a people, have been consistently disparaged. Apart from physical violence, conquered and conqueror have continued to be competitors for land and jobs and power, parties to a constant economic conflict which has found expression in litigation, dispossessions, hotly contested elections and the mutual disparagement which inevitably accompanies a situation of this kind. Throughout this struggle, the Anglo-Americans have possessed every advantage: in numbers and wealth, arms and machines.[4]

By its own internal laws, capitalism could not miss the opportunity to take advantage of such a numerous and cheap labor force. At the same time that it derived great benefits from the utilization of this labor force, it denied economic, social, and political equality to the Mexican. This denial in turn assured the capitalists that the Mexicans would constitute a group that could be exploited in the future, a group that would yield higher profits than the Anglo workers. The Anglo workers have received a share of the benefits of capitalism and thus have ended up defending the system that bought them. They have become loyal accomplices of capitalism, both in the exploitation of minority groups at home and in the exploitation of Third World peoples outside the United States.

"The Mexican problem" has its roots in the economic base of the United States, the capitalist structure, which both frustrates the development of the Mexican people—the nationality—and creates fierce economic exploitation and a policy of discrimination in all aspects of life. Lack of education, cultural contrasts, and linguistic problems are intimately related to that situation.

The Destiny of the Chicano National Minority

A correct understanding of how a society develops and the relationships that govern that development can enable us to envision the future. The United States is the center of the world imperialist system, the home base of a vast and powerful economic, military, and political empire. This situation has produced a radical change in class relations within U.S. society; the working class has been divested of its class consciousness by means of the benefits it gets from U.S. exploitation of the Third World.

In our opinion, this situation is by no means fatal or eternal. In proportion to the growth of revolutionary struggle in the Third World, internal and external contradictions will become more acute and will produce inevitable changes in class relations in the United States. The future of racial and national minorities in the United States is intimately and inevitably linked to the destiny of the society as a whole. But because of the position of these minorities as doubly exploited groups, the very real possibility exists that Blacks, Mexicans, Puerto Ricans, Asians, and Indians may play a most important role as the instigators of revolutionary social change in the United States.

We must recognize that U.S. society at present cannot integrate or assimilate the national and racial minorities. These minorities must therefore look for their own way to a truly human kind of life, and that way is the total transformation of U.S. society. In our opinion, no changes will be made in favor of the minorities so long as the system that gives rise to racial and national problems exists. Until the capitalist structure of the United States changes, the minorities as well as millions of poor Anglos will grow up in a world where drugs, crime, prostitution, and the most dehumanizing alienation is their daily bread. *So long as capitalism is the reigning system in the United States, absolute inequality in all fields important to human life will prevail.*

Bound together by a life of common suffering, bitterness, frustration, and despair, the racial and national minorities together with the most progressive white sectors must initiate change in the present state of affairs. *The union of Blacks with Mexicans and Puerto Ricans is a historical necessity which must be brought into being.* The Chicano people will join their forces with the forces that are fighting for revolutionary change. Like their legendary heroes of the past, the Chicanos will prove that their main dream is that of making Aztlán a place for free men and women.

Notes

1. McWilliams, *North from Mexico*, p. 207.
2. Joseph Stalin, "Marxism and the National Question," in *Selected Works* (Davis, Cal.: Cardinal, 1971), p. 53.
3. Ibid., p. 68.
4. McWilliams, *North from Mexico*, p. 132.

Appendix:
Tables

Table 1

Emigration from Mexico to the United States, 1900–1968

Period	Mexican emigrants	% of total
1900–1909	23,991	.3
1910–1919	224,705	3.0
1920–1929	436,733	10.1
1930–1939	27,937	3.9
1940–1949	54,290	6.3
1950–1959	293,469	11.7
1960–1968	386,892	13.4

Source: Leo Grebler et al., *The Mexican-American People* (New York: Free Press, 1970).

Table 2

Population of Mexican Origin in Southwest from 1930–1970

Year	1930	1940	1950	1960	1970
Number	1,282,883	1,570,740	2,281,720	3,464,999	4,549,000

Sources: U.S., Department of Commerce, *Census of Population*, and U.S., Bureau of the Census, *Current Population Report*, Series P-20, no. 238 (July 1972).

Table 3

Each State's Percentage of the
Total Population of Mexican Origin
in the Southwest

State	1930	1940	1950	1960
Arizona	8.8	6.3	5.6	5.6
California	28.6	26.4	33.2	41.2
Colorado	4.4	5.8	5.2	4.5
New Mexico	4.6	14.2	10.9	7.8
Texas	46.4	47.3	45.0	40.9
	92.8	100.0	99.9	100.0

Table 4

*Percentage of Total Population of the Southwest
Which Is of Mexican Origin,
from 1950 to 1972*

Year	1950	1960	1972
Percent	10.9	11.8	12.3

Sources: U.S., Department of Commerce, *Census of Population*, and U.S., Bureau of the Census, *Current Population Report*, Series P-20, no. 238 (July 1972).

Table 5

*Distribution of Population of Mexican Origin by Age Group,
as of March 1972*

Population of Mexican origin		Total U.S. population	
Age group	Percent of total	Age group	Percent of total
0–5	13.4	0–5	8.5
5–9	15.0	5–9	9.2
10–17	20.2	10–17	16.0
18–19	4.3	18–19	3.6
20–24	8.3	20–24	8.4
25–34	13.3	25–34	12.9
35–44	10.8	35–44	11.0
45–54	7.5	45–54	11.4
55–64	3.9	55–64	9.2
65 and over	3.2	65 and over	9.7

Source: U.S., Bureau of the Census, *Current Population Report*, Series P-20, no. 238 (July 1972).

Table 6

*Occupation of Men and Women of Mexican Origin
as of November 1969 by Percent*

Occupation	Men		Women	
	Mexican	Total population	Mexican	Total population
White-collar work	18.5	41.4	37.7	60.7
Blue-collar work	64.4	47.1	29.6	16.1
Farm work	8.7	5.1	1.2	1.7
Service work	8.4	6.5	31.5	21.5

Source: U.S., Bureau of the Census, *Current Population Report*, Series P-20, no. 213 (February 1971).

Table 7

Median Annual Income of Men in the Southwest in 1960

	Mexican origin	Anglo	Black
Urban and rural areas	$2,768	$4,815	$2,435
Urban areas only	$3,156	$5,134	$2,738

Table 8

Family Income of Households of Mexican Origin as of March 1972

Total income	Families of Mexican origin earning that income (in percent)	Families in general population earning that income (in percent)
Under $3,000	14.9	8.3
$ 3,000 to $3,999	9.2	4.8
$ 4,000 to $4,999	7.1	5.4
$ 5,000 to $5,999	8.3	5.7
$ 6,000 to $6,999	7.0	5.5
$ 7,000 to $7,999	7.1	6.2
$ 8,000 to $9,999	15.1	12.3
$10,000 to $11,999	11.8	12.5
$12,000 to $14,999	10.2	14.4
$15,000 to $24,999	8.6	19.5
$25,000 and over	0.5	5.3

Source: U.S., Bureau of the Census, *Current Population Report*, Series P-20, no. 238 (July 1972).

II
Readings

1

Toward an Operational Definition of the Mexican-American

Fernando Peñalosa

The sociological study of the Mexican-American, until very recently almost the exclusive province of Anglo sociologists, is about to be launched into a new period of development that should certainly produce more fruitful, more realistic, and more relevant data and conclusions than have previously been forthcoming. Before we move into this new period, however, we would be well advised to map out somewhat more carefully the population we are going to study. In developing a relatively new field it is not so important to attempt to produce immediately the right answers as it is to ask the right questions. If we ask simple questions we may get simple and probably misleading answers, particularly since our subject is not at all simple, but exceedingly complex. Mexican-Americans may constitute one of the most heterogeneous ethnic groups ever to be studied by sociologists. With reference to the scholarly study of the Mexican-American we would be well advised to stop trying to find the "typical" or "true," and seek rather to establish the range of variation. Generalizations extrapolated from the community in which a Chicano writer happened to grow up or which an Anglo sociologist or anthropologist happened to have studied can be particularly misleading.

It is furthermore essential that we avoid simplistic either-or types of questions, such as, Are Chicanos a people or not?, Do they have a distinctive culture or not?, or, Is there such a thing existentially as the Mexican-American community or not? Realistically we are handicapped in attempting to answer these types of inquiries in which the alternatives are already implicitly limited by the question itself. A much more productive approach might be rather to consider prefixing our questions with a phrase such as "to what extent . . ." so that we ask to what extent do Mexican-Americans constitute a stratum, possess a distinct subculture, etc.

Scholars, both Chicano and Anglo, have furthermore spent countless hours debating the question of the correct name for our group, and then attempting to define the entity for which the supposedly correct name stands. Perhaps the time has come to move beyond terminological and definitional polemics to an examination of some of the dimensions along which we might explore our subject in an attempt better to understand its character.[1]

The method of procedure in this paper will be as follows. A series of questions will be asked about the Mexican-American population. An attempt will be made to answer each one, based on the writer's admittedly limited perception of the current state of knowledge, and to point out some possible lines of future research along that dimension. *Some* day, when we have approximately adequate answers to the questions posed, we *may* have a more or less acceptable operational definition of the Mexican-American. By way of overview, these are the questions which will be discussed:

1. To what extent do Mexican-Americans constitute a separate racial entity?

2. To what extent do Mexican-Americans conceive of themselves as belonging to a separate ethnic group?

3. To what extent do Mexican-Americans have a separate or distinct culture?

4. To what extent do Mexican-Americans constitute an identifiable stratum in society?

5. To what extent is it realistic to speak of Mexican-American communities?

6. To what extent are differences in historical antecedents reflected among Mexican-Americans?

7. To what extent are regional socioeconomic differences significant among Mexican-Americans?[2]

Let us then direct our attention to each of these questions in turn.

To what extent do Mexican-Americans constitute a separate racial entity?

A goodly number of Mexican-Americans and others are confused as to the biological nature of this particular group. An Anglo-American may carelessly divide people into whites, Negroes, and Mexicans, or a Chicano may assertively speak of "La Raza."[3] The recently increasing use of the term "brown" similarly represents pride in the group's presumed racial distinctiveness, analogous not only to the Negroes' newly found blackness but also to "La Raza Cósmica" of José Vasconcelos. Although most Mexican-Americans are of mixed Spanish, Indian (both Southwestern and Mexican), and Negro descent, a large proportion are not physically distinct from the majority American population; hence the group as a whole cannot be characterized in terms of race.[4] "Race" is essentially furthermore a nineteenth-century notion which is rapidly becoming obsolete in physical anthropology and related disciplines. In any case, biological differences as such are no concern of the sociologist; only the ways in which notions of race influence people's behavior concern him. The topic of our discussion is therefore what social scientists refer to as socially supposed races. Regardless of whatever mythology may be involved, however, if the majority group considers Mexican-Americans as a race, and insists therefore on continuing to treat them in a discriminatory fashion, then the consequences are nonetheless real: not only the deprivation and segregation, but as the progress of the Chicano movement has shown, racial pride. Not all the consequences of racism are necessarily negative.

Some historical perspective is needed here. With reference to color discrimination it was noted by Manuel Gamio that in the 1920s dark-skinned Mexicans suffered about the same type of discrimination as Negroes, but that medium-complected Mexicans were able to use second-class public facilities. Even light-brown skinned Mexicans were excluded from high-class facilities, while "white" Mexicans might be freely admitted, especially if they spoke fluent English.[5] To what extent is such a type of scale still applied in public facilities or in other areas of public and private life, and what social factors affect its application? Furthermore, we might well examine the extent to which differences in physical appearances are socially significant to Mexican-Americans themselves. The fact that we live in a racist society where the primary factor affecting a person's status and life chances has always been the color of his skin, means that it is unrealistic to attempt to sweep an unpleasant situation under the carpet and pretend it does not exist.

To what extent do Mexican-Americans conceive of themselves as belonging to a separate ethnic group?

Tentatively at least we might characterize an ethnic group as a subpopulation which shares a common ancestry and which is distinguished by a way of life or culture which is significantly different in one or more respects from that of the majority of the population, which regards it as an out-group. Do Mexican-Americans conceive of themselves in this manner? If they thus conceive of themselves, what is the degree of separateness perceived? It depends of course on whom you ask. But it may be hypothesized that answers would probably fall along a spectrum or continuum, of which it is not too difficult to identify three principal segments: those at the extremes, and one at or near the center.

These segments can be characterized according to varying self-conceptions and variations in self-identity. At one extreme are those who acknowledge the fact of their Mexican descent but for whom this fact constitutes neither a particularly positive nor a particularly negative value, because it plays a very unimportant part in their lives and their self-conception. At or near the middle of this putative continuum are those for whom being of Mexican ancestry is something of which they are constantly conscious and which looms importantly as part of their self-conception. Their Mexican descent may constitute for them a positive value, a negative value, or more generally an ambiguous blend of the two. At the other end of the continuum are those who are not only acutely aware of their Mexican identity and descent but are committed to the defense of Mexican-American subcultural values, and strive to work actively for the betterment of their people. Tentatively I would like to suggest, without any implication as to their "correctness," that the terms "Americans of Mexican ancestry," "Mexican-Americans," and "Chicanos," are sometimes used for those who closely resemble the three types suggested.

Research is needed to determine whether indeed such a continuum can be identified, and if so, what are the proportions of persons falling at various points along its length, and with what other social indices these positions are associated. Sample surveys would seem to be one of the most direct ways of attacking this problem.[6]

To what extent do Mexican-Americans have a separate or distinct culture?

Mexican-American culture or subculture, whatever its precise nature, composition, and structure, if such are even determinable, appears to be a product of multiple origins, as one would expect in light of its history. The focus of its synthesis and emergence is of course the barrio and it is here and not toward Mexico where we must focus our primary attention. At the same time we should not minimize differences between the way of life of Chicanos residing inside and of those residing outside the barrio.

Tentatively it may be suggested that the chief sources of Mexican-American culture are four in number. First, there is the initially overriding but subsequently attenuated influence of what is usually called "traditional" Mexican culture, the way of life brought by most of the immigrants from Mexico during several centuries.[7]

Second, there is the initially weak but subsequently growing influence of the surrounding majority American culture. Mexican-Americans are subject to approximately the same educational system and mass media communication as are other Americans and participate to varying extents in the economic, social, intellectual, and religious life of the broader society. A careful comparison of the way of life of persons of Mexican descent in the United States with those of Mexico will help substantiate the notion that the former are first and foremost "Americans," and only secondarily "Mexican-Americans."

A third source of influence upon Mexican-American culture is class influence. The fact that the bulk of the Mexican-American population has been concentrated at the lower socioeconomic levels of the society means that some aspects of Mexican-American culture may have their source in behavior characteristic generally of lower-class people regardless of ethnic group. Thus, for example, the alleged relatively high crime rate (at least for certain types of crimes) among Mexican-Americans can perhaps best be explained in terms of social class rather than ethnicity, as well as in terms of the relative youth of the group as a whole and differential law enforcement practices. Apart from the question of Anglo discrimination, insensitivity, and incompetence, Mexican-American problems in education seem to be as much class problems as they are cultural problems. Educational studies comparing lower-class Chicano students with middle-class Anglos are as methodologically faulty as they are socially pernicious. Neither must it be forgotten that class discrimination is as real in this country as racial or ethnic discrimination.

The fourth source of influence on Mexican-American culture results from the minority status of its bearers. The term "minority" is not properly a numerical concept (Chicanos outnumber Anglos in East Los Angeles), but rather a term suggesting that the group has less than its share of political, economic, and social power vis-à-vis the majority population and hence suffers from educational, social, occupational, and other economic disadvantages mediated through the processes of prejudice, discrimination, and segregation. Inasmuch as the concept of culture basically refers to the sum total of techniques a people has in coping with and adapting to its physical and social environment, there have been developed some special cultural responses among Mexican-Americans to their minority status, as occurs among members of other minority groups. These responses may be viewed as very important components of the admittedly heterogeneous and ill-defined Chicano subculture. An obvious example of this sort of trait is the Chicano movement itself, which is both a response to the majority culture and society, and an outstanding component of Chicano culture itself. But even here the matter gets complicated, for it is necessary to recognize that the movement has borrowed at least some of its goals, values, techniques, and strategies from both the Black and Anglo civil rights movements.

It is suggested therefore that Mexican-American culture is a multidimensional phenomenon and must be studied in terms of these four dimensions at least (there may be more), as well as in terms of its historical, regional, and ecological variants. It is highly unlikely that all the various strands will ever be completely unraveled and laid out neatly side by side for us to see, but neither must we lose sight of the heterogeneous origins of Mexican-American culture, the nature of the varying continuing influences on it, and its continuously changing nature, as we seek to ascertain its differential dispersal, influence, and persistence among persons of Mexican descent in this country.

To what extent do Mexican-Americans constitute an identifiable stratum in society?

A number of social scientists who have studied the relations between Mexican-Americans and Anglo-Americans in the Southwest have described these relations as being "caste-like." [8] That is, the nature of inter-ethnic relations was said to bear some resemblance to the relations between castes in India and elsewhere. In the United States the situation which undoubtedly most closely resembles a color caste system is the traditional pattern of race relations in the South, with its supposedly superordinate white caste and subordinate Negro caste.

Although Mexican-Anglo relations have never been as rigid as Black-white relations, there may still have been a resemblance, particularly in certain communities, strong enough to characterize them as "semi-caste," "quasi-caste," or "caste-like." That is, there would be manifested a strong degree of segregation, blocking of entrance to certain occupations, political impotence, ritual avoidance, and taboos on inter-marriage stemming from notions of "racial" or "color" differences. Intermarriage is an important criterion, for marriage implies social equality between partners. The idea that Mexicans and Mexican-Americans are not whites was certainly more prevalent before the World War II period, or at least people expressed the idea more frequently without worrying whether or not anyone might take offense. The current situation in this regard is unclear.[9] It may be that the continuing low rate of intermarriage, the tacit or explicit superior-inferior nature of ethnic relations, and the concentration of Mexican-Americans in certain jobs and their virtual exclusion from others, means that Mexican-Anglo relations still approximate semi-caste, although increasingly less so.

If Anglo-Mexican relations appear to be moving away from a caste basis to a class basis, and the evidence is definitely pointing in this direction, the internal stratification of the Mexican-American population looms increasingly more important. With a few exceptions, our knowledge of Mexican-American stratification has had to depend so far primarily on the rather impressionistic accounts of a handful of Anglo social scientists. We know that, generally speaking, Mexican-American rural populations have less differentiated social class structures than the urban ones, that is, the status spread is greater in the city than in the country. We know some of the variables associated with socioeconomic status and self and community perception. Much more we do not know.

Impressionistic accounts and reworking of U.S. Census data in the manner of the UCLA Mexican-American Study Project have not been enough. Careful original sample surveys to study the interrelations of "objective" stratification variables as well as the study of the "subjective" perceptions by Chicanos of their own internal stratification systems are urgently needed. Only thus will the myth of the class homogeneity of the Mexican-American population be thoroughly discredited and its heterogeneity adequately documented.

To what extent is it realistic to speak of Mexican-American communities?

One badly neglected area of research is the extent to which Mexican-Americans have a feeling of belonging to an identifiable Mexican-American community and the extent to which their participation in its organizations and other community activities enable us to identify leadership roles and a social structure as well as a body of sentiment. Regional and ecological considerations are of primary importance here. Degree of community feeling and participation undoubtedly varies as among such places as East Los Angeles, Pamona, Tucson, Chicago, or Hidalgo County, Texas, to mention but a few. It varies between those who live in the barrio and those who live outside. Rural-urban differences are likewise significant. Rural Mexican-Americans were never able to establish true communities in California, for example, because of Anglo pressures and because of the migratory work patterns of most of the people, according to Ernesto Galarza.[10] The range and variation of "communityness" must be empirically studied, not assumed a priori, both within populations and among a sample of different locales reflecting the differential impact of relevant regional and ecological variables.

To what extent are differences in historical antecedents reflected among Mexican-Americans?

To a certain extent this question foreshadows the succeeding one inasmuch as the principal regional variations have emerged because of different historical antecedents, and hence it is possible to separate analytically but not empirically the geographical and historical dimensions.

The Mexican-American population in the United States from 1848 down to the present has been continually expanded and renewed by immigration both legal and illegal from Mexico, a continually changing Mexico. Mexican immigrants came, for example, before the Revolution, during the Revolution, shortly after the Revolution, and more recently, each coming from a somewhat different Mexico. Those coming in at the present time as permanent residents come for the most part from a Mexico vastly more industrialized, urbanized, modernized, and educated than the Mexico of our fathers or grandfathers. How well have immigrants from different periods of Mexico's history, and their children, fared in the United States? What have been the differential rates of mobility and/or assimilation? We should also raise questions about generational differences, and with reference to the differential composition of Mexican-American local populations in terms of their historical antecedents. How are these kinds of differences associated with significant social indices, rates of acculturation, and self-perception and self-identity variables?

To what extent are regional socioeconomic differences significant among Mexican-Americans?

A number of Mexican-American regional subcultures can probably be identified. The historical and geographical factors affecting the emergence of these sub-varieties are of crucial importance in understanding their present nature. It is important to realize, for example, that the Hispanos of New Mexico and Colorado evolved their culture in isolated mountain villages fairly remote from Anglo civilization; that the Texas Mexicans are not only concentrated along the border but are also located geographically in the South with its unique tradition of discrimination and prejudice; whereas the Chicanos of Southern California have been caught up in a changing situation of rapid urban growth.

In all areas of the Southwest, the shift from rural to urban has been a highly significant trend. The overwhelming majority of Southwestern Mexican-Americans now live in urban areas. These Mexican-American urban settlements have grown primarily through migration from the countryside, so that the bulk of the adult residents of those communities have not yet completely adjusted to urban life. The kinds of problems they face therefore are quite different from those they had to face in the small towns and rural areas from which they came. Simple agricultural skills are no longer enough for the security of employment. The kinds of job opportunities available are primarily of an industrial nature and increasingly require a high degree of either manual dexterity or intellectual skills or both. The needs of automation are furthermore constantly raising the level of skills required in order to compete successfully in the job market. So the urban Mexican-American is pushed further and further away from pre-industrial skills, habits, and attitudes and directly into the modern industrial social order with all its complexities and problems.

At the opposite extreme, Mexican-Americans in such a place as rural Texas score the lowest on all the social measures. It is in this area that the permanent residences of many migratory agricultural laborers are concentrated. There is perhaps less social differentiation of Mexican-Americans here than in any other area of the Southwest, and the most vigorous preservation of so-called traditional Mexican rural culture.

The Spanish-Americans, Hispanos, "Manitos," or "mejicanos," are the descendants of the original racially mixed but Europeanized settlers of New Mexico and southern Colorado, when this area was under Spanish rule, but administered and colonized from Mexico. Traditionally most of the Hispanos lived in isolated rural areas and were economically and socially handicapped. In recent years they have become increasingly urbanized as many have been forced off their lands by the more competitive Anglo farmers, or as mines were closed. Many Hispanos left New Mexico and Colorado during the World War II and postwar periods. Many came and continue to come to Southern California and other areas of high urbanization. Here we have another case of attempting to unravel the strands, as Chicano urban populations are increasing in heterogeneity with reference to interstate geographical origins. The sociological study of the Mexican-American should include both the *systematic* comparative examination of regional variants of the admittedly hard to define and identify Chicano culture and community (and *not* just a series of monographic reports, each one on a separate community), as well as the way in which these differences are being gradually obliterated in the urban milieu.[11]

In summary, seven questions were posed with reference to the Chicano population, some tentative answers were given, and some areas for future research indicated. It is not the writer's intention to imply that a series of adequately documented answers to these questions would constitute the corpus of Chicano sociology. There are a number of other extremely important unmentioned questions and topics which are obviously part of such a sociology, such as those relating to family life, value systems, power relations, bilingualism, educational questions, and many others. Rather, the explicit intention and hope is that the answers to these questions will help in the formulation of a sociological definition of our subject population before we tackle the multitude of difficult intellectual and social questions which lie ahead of us.

Notes

1. The terms "Mexican-American" and "Chicano" are used here for convenience as equivalent and interchangeable, without any implication of their "correctness" or of the "correctness"

of any other term or terms that might have been used in their place.

2. The careful reader will have detected that the writer's philosophical bias is strongly nominalistic, that is, that he conceives of "culture," "community," "ethnic group," etc., not as "things," but rather as labels which refer to abstractions conjured up by the social scientist or others as a convenience in handling the data they are trying to understand. For example, the latest issue of *El Chicano*, a newspaper published in San Bernardino, carries the headline "Mexican Community Demands Dismissal of Judge Chargin." This is a figure of speech, of course, inasmuch as if the community is indeed an abstraction, it cannot demand anything; only individuals or organized groups can demand.

3. Readers of this journal are undoubtedly acquainted with the fact that throughout the Spanish-speaking world Columbus Day is referred to as "El Día de la Raza," the word "raza" in this context referring to all persons of Hispanic culture, as it does in the motto of the National Autonomous University of Mexico: "Por mi raza hablará el espíritu." Nevertheless, in social matters, words mean what their users *want* them to mean.

4. Cf. Marcus Goldstein, *Demographic and Bodily Changes in Descendants of Mexican Immigrants* (Austin, Texas: Institute of Latin American Studies, University of Texas, 1943), and Gonzalo Aguirre Beltrán, *La Población Negra de México 1519–1810* (Mexico, D. F.: Eds. Fuente Cultural, 1946).

5. Manuel Gamio, *Mexican Immigration to the United States* (Chicago: University of Chicago Press, 1930), p. 53.

6. The writer is currently carrying out a random-sample survey of the Mexican-American population of San Bernardino, California, with reference to internal social stratification, self-identification, and perception of community and subculture. Hopefully the results will throw some light on these questions.

7. The pitfalls of stereotyping in this area are very great, as so ably pointed out by Octavio I. Romano-V., "The Anthropology and Sociology of the Mexican Americans," *El Grito* 2 (Fall 1968), pp. 13–26.

8. Walter Goldschmidt, *As You Sow* (New York: Harcourt, Brace

and Co., 1947), p. 59; Paul Schuster Taylor, *An American-Mexican Frontier, Nueces County, Texas* (Chapel Hill: University of North Carolina Press, 1934); Ruth D. Tuck, *Not With the Fist: Mexican-Americans in a Southwest City* (New York: Harcourt, Brace and Co., 1946), p. 44; Thomas E. Lasswell, "Status Stratification in a Selected Community," Ph.D. diss., University of Southern California, 1953; Robert B. Rogers, "Perception of the Power Structure by Social Class in a California Community," Ph.D. diss., University of Southern California, 1962; James B. Watson and Julián Samora, "Subordinate Leadership in a Bi-cultural Community," *American Sociological Review* 19 (August 1954), pp. 413–421; Ozzie Simmons, "Americans and Mexican Americans in South Texas," Ph.D. diss., Harvard University, 1952; William H. Madsen, *The Mexican-Americans of South Texas* (New York: Holt, Rinehart and Winston, 1964).

It may be argued that since the authors of all these studies are Anglos they may have had a slanted view of the situation, yet it should be understood they are reporting Anglo residents' perceptions of the social barriers they themselves have set up.

9. After the 1930 Census, in which Mexicans were listed as a separate "race," persons of Mexican descent were subsequently put back into the "white" category largely because the Mexican-American leaders of that time insisted Mexicans were "white." Similarly the Chicano population is substantially the same as the 1950 and 1960 Census category, "White persons of Spanish surname." Understandably therefore the recent emphasis on "brown" and "La Raza" has some Anglos confused. With reference to the possible relevance of the caste model, it should be pointed out that the nature of the discrimination against Chicanos has been primarily social rather than legal, as has been the case for Blacks in the South.

10. Lecture in the University of California Extension Series "The Mexican American in Transition," Ontario, California, Spring 1967.

11. One of the findings of the writer's "Spanish-surname" sample survey of Pomona was that in every case in which a household contained a "Spanish-American" adult, that person was married to a "Mexican-American." It may be hypothesized on the

basis of this admittedly flimsy evidence that in urban Southern California Hispanos are more likely to marry children or grandchildren of Mexican immigrants than they are Hispanos because there are no real barriers between the two groups and the satistical odds are therefore against the endogamy of the smaller group. To what extent this may be true of other areas of the country it would be hazardous to guess.

2

El Plan de Delano

The Plan of Delano was announced by the National Farmworkers' Association (now United Farmworkers' Organizing Committee) in March 1966 during the farmworkers' peregrinación—pilgrimage—on foot from Delano to Sacramento, the state capital of California. Thousands of people joined in the 300-mile walk at the height of the Delano grape strike. The Plan was like a declaration of independence, of liberation.

We, the undersigned, gathered in pilgrimage to the capital of the state in Sacramento, in penance for all the failings of farmworkers as free and sovereign men, do solemnly declare before the civilized world which judges our actions, and before the nation to which we belong, the propositions we have formulated to end the injustice that oppresses us.

We are conscious of the historical significance of our pilgrimage. It is clearly evident that our path travels through a valley well known to all Mexican farmworkers. We know all of these towns of Delano, Fresno, Madera, Modesto, Stockton, and Sacramento, because along this very same road, in this very same valley, the Mexican race has sacrificed itself for the last hundred years. Our sweat and our blood have fallen on this land to make other men rich. Our wages and working

107

conditions have been determined from above, because irresponsible legislators who could have helped us have supported the rancher's argument that the plight of the farmworker was a "special case." They saw the obvious effects of an unjust system, starvation wages, contractors, day hauls, forced migration, sickness, and subhuman conditions.

The farmworker has been abandoned to his own fate— without representation, without power—subject to the mercy and caprice of the rancher.

We are suffering. We have suffered unnumbered ills and crimes in the name of the law of the land. Our men, women, and children have suffered not only the basic brutality of stoop labor, and the most obvious injustices of the system; they have also suffered the desperation of knowing that that system caters to the greed of callous men and not to our needs.

Now we will suffer for the purpose of ending the poverty, the misery, and the injustice, with the hope that our children will not be exploited as we have been. They have imposed hungers on us, and now we hunger for justice. We draw strength from the very despair in which we have been forced to live. WE SHALL ENDURE!

This pilgrimage is a witness to the suffering we have seen for generations. The penance we accept symbolizes the suffering we shall have in order to bring justice to these same towns, to this same valley. This is the beginning of a social movement in fact and not in pronouncements.

We seek our basic God-given rights as human beings. Because we have suffered—and are not afraid to suffer—in order to survive, we are ready to give up everything, even our lives, in our fight for social justice. We shall do it without violence because that is our destiny.

To the ranchers and to all those who oppose us we say, in the words of Benito Juárez, "Respect for another's rights is the meaning of peace."

We seek the support of all political groups, and the

protection of the government, which is also our government. But we are tired of words, of betrayals, of indifference. To the politicians we say that the years are gone when the farmworker said nothing and did nothing to help himself. From this movement shall spring leaders who shall understand us, lead us, be faithful to us, and we shall elect them to represent us. We shall be heard!

We seek, and have, the support of the Church in what we do. At the head of the pilgrimage we carry the Virgin of Guadalupe because she is ours, all ours, Patroness of the Mexican people. We also carry the Sacred Cross and the Star of David because we are not sectarians, and because we ask the help and prayers of all religions. All men are brothers, sons of the same God; that is why we say to all men of good will, in the words of Pope Leo XIII, "Everyone's first duty is to protect the workers from the greed of speculators who use human beings as instruments to provide themselves with money. It is neither just nor human to oppress with excessive work to the point where their minds become enfeebled and their bodies worn out." God shall not abandon us!

We shall unite. We have learned the meaning of unity. We know why these United States are just that—united. The strength of the poor is also in union. We know that the poverty of the Mexican or Filipino worker in California is the same as that of all farmworkers across the country, the Negroes and poor whites, the Puerto Ricans, Japanese and Arabians; in short, all of the races that comprise the oppressed minorities of the United States. The majority of the people on our pilgrimage are of Mexican descent, but the triumph of our race depends on a national association of farmworkers. We must get together and bargain collectively. We must use the only strength that we have, the force of our numbers; the ranchers are few, we are many. United we shall stand!

We shall pursue the Revolution we have proposed. We are sons of the Mexican Revolution, a revolution of the poor seeking bread and justice. Our revolution shall not be an armed one, but we want the order which now exists to be undone, and that a new social order replace it.

We are poor, we are humble, and our only choice is to strike in those ranches where we are not treated with the respect we deserve as working men, where our rights as free and sovereign men are not recognized. We do not want the paternalism of the ranchers; we do not want the contractor; we do not want charity at the price of our dignity. We want to be equal with all the working men in the nation; we want a just wage, better working conditions, a decent future for our children. To those who oppose us, be they ranchers, police, politicians, or speculators, we say that we are going to continue fighting until we die, or we win. We shall overcome!

Across the San Joaquin Valley, across California, across the entire Southwest of the United States, wherever there are Mexican people, wherever there are farmworkers, our movement is spreading like flames across a dry plain. Our pilgrimage is the match that will light our cause for all farmworkers to see what is happening here, so that they may do as we have done.

The time has come for the liberation of the poor farmworker. History is on our side. May the strike go on! Viva la causa!

3

Causes of Land Loss Among The Spanish-Americans in Northern New Mexico

Clark S. Knowlton

The Spanish-Americans are unique among the various ethnic groups found in the United States in that they share certain historical experiences with the American Indians. Like the Indians, they were conquered in war and forced to become citizens of the United States. Like the Indians, their personal and property rights were guaranteed to them by a treaty that was broken shortly after it was signed. Unlike the Indians, they at no time have ever enjoyed the minimal and ambiguous protection offered the Indians by a government bureau and by interested private organizations.

They were left defenseless before the invading, dynamic, ruthless, legalistic, lawless, and competitive Anglo-American civilization of the nineteenth century that did nothing to prepare them for adequate citizenship; stripped them of most of their land; reduced them to the situation of a conquered people without enforceable rights; and left them in extreme poverty.

Under Spanish and Mexican rule there were three basic forms of land settlement in New Mexico. The first and most important was the community grant and charter. When the

This essay originally appeared in *Rocky Mountain Social Science Journal*, April 5, 1963. Reprinted with permission.

grant was awarded, the village site was first laid out with plaza, church site, and residential lots delineated. House sites and irrigation land were distributed by lot. Each member family received a title to its residential site and irrigated land plus the right to graze livestock and to cut timber upon the village commons.

The second type of grant leading to the formation of a rural village was the proprietary grant made to a prominent individual who promised to secure settlers, distribute residential sites and irrigated land, provide for the building of canals and dams, construct a church, and secure a priest. The proprietor was the patron of the village. He had certain economic rights and could call upon the villagers to assist him militarily. This type of grant was frequently made in areas exposed to Indian raids.

The *sitio* was the third type of land grant. It was usually a large personal grant made to a prominent individual in return for military, economic, or political services. The individual to secure title was required to settle on the land. In the course of time as descendants of the original grantee multiplied, many *sitios* became in essence community grants.

Another form of common land settlement among the Spanish-Americans during the Mexican period and early stages of American occupation was what could be called a social compact. A group of villagers, moving from an overcrowded village into an area possessing usable land, established a village that might or might not contain a plaza, divided up the irrigated land and residential sites by lot, and grazed the nearby range. No effort was made to obtain a legal charter or to record land rights.

The American conquest found the majority of Spanish-Americans living in small, autonomous, self-sufficient farm villages based upon subsistence agriculture and grazing activities, providing for their wants through handicrafts and barter. Illiterate, the villagers lived from generation to generation relatively independent, isolated, and little touched by commerce or by a money economy.

The swelling land conflicts that marked New Mexican history from 1879 to 1930 were perhaps inevitable. They grew out of the quite distinct and conflicting patterns of land ownership and land use. Among the Spanish-Americans the habitual use of the land was more important than recorded titles. The vast majority of them were illiterate. Most families made little attempt to preserve whatever written charters or land titles that they might have received. Land ownership was not based primarily upon a written right but upon traditional and recognized rights of occupancy respected by their neighbors. There developed a tacit division of the land based upon land use and prior settlement, kinship, and the belief that everyone should have access to land in order to earn a living. Grant lands were usually immune from taxation, and a tax on land was beyond the remotest conception of the Spanish-Americans. The financial needs of the Spanish and Mexican authorities were met by tariffs and by taxes upon harvests and livestock increase. If harvests were poor, taxes were remitted. There did not exist any authoritative system of land survey and land boundaries were vague and imprecise.

Although the government of the United States committed itself through the Treaty of Guadalupe Hidalgo to protect property and civic rights of the Spanish-Americans, they were treated as a conquered and subject people. Even though the number of Anglo-Americans in New Mexico before the Civil War was small, land losses began. A Catholic Sister of Charity resident in the Territory during this period stated that:

> In the early years of Anglo settlement in New Mexico the unsuspicious and naive Spanish Americans were victimized on every hand. When the men from the states came out west to dispossess the poor natives of their lands, they used many

subterfuges. One was to offer the owner of the land a handful of silver coins for the small service of making a mark on a paper. The mark was a cross which was accepted as a signature and by which the unsuspecting natives deeded away their lands. By this means many a poor family was robbed of all its possessions.

By the 1880s, the number of Americans in New Mexico had increased considerably. The two groups of Anglos that had the most harmful impact upon the Spanish Americans— the lawyers and the ranchers—began entering the Territory of New Mexico in large numbers during this period. One authority estimated that one out of every ten Anglos in New Mexico in this period was a lawyer. Known to some Spanish-Americans as black vultures, they managed to thoroughly entrap these people in the subtle legal technicalities and the mysteries of the Anglo law that even today are regarded as a dark and dangerous jungle by the Spanish-Americans.

The lawyers were quick to see what large fortunes could be made from the obscure and unregistered titles of the unsuspecting Spanish-Americans. Within a short period after the Civil War, the Territory of New Mexico fell into the hands of groups of unscrupulous lawyers cooperating closely together for mutual profit. Many of these lawyers within a few years became wealthy and could be counted among the largest landholders of the United States. The activities of these rings have remained unstudied and in the dark recesses of New Mexican history. They counted among their numbers, governors, state supreme court justices, land recorders, surveyors, and other political officials in New Mexico and Washington, D.C.

The Anglo-Americans with their system of sharp, well-defined land boundaries, registered titles, a land system based upon the idea that if there are no records there is no defensible title, and an economic system founded on competition, a ruthless struggle for wealth, and a permissive lawlessness found it impossible to either respect the Spanish-Americans or their political or economic rights. Furthermore, with the immigration into New Mexico of large numbers of Texans, the harsh Texan attitude toward Spanish-speaking groups began to spread among all levels of Anglo-American society in New Mexico and in government circles in Washington, D.C.

The first political shadows cast upon Spanish-American landholdings was the congressional act of July 22, 1854, that reserved for Congress the right to pass upon private land claims in New Mexico by direct legislative enactment. No provisions were made for appeal, adverse proceedings, or for surveying boundaries of claimed tracts. All land claimants under Spanish and Mexican grants had to pay for their own surveys, to undertake and carry forward long and expensive legal procedures and litigation. Government officials both in Santa Fe and in Washington, D.C., usually endeavored to whittle down acreage and to throw out genuine Spanish-American land grants on the fiction that they did not have a legally perfect title. As Ralph E. Twitchell reports: "No claimant could secure congressional affirmation of his title unless he was able to spend a long period of time in Washington and was abundantly equipped with funds to organize a lobby to smooth the passage of a private act confirming his land claim."

A Spanish-American knowing little English, possessing no funds, unfamiliar with Washington, D.C. and with American political and moral folkways and mores was almost helpless against Anglo contestants.

The situation was worsened further by the fact that only two federal land offices in early New Mexican history were established in New Mexico; one in Santa Fe and the other in Las Cruces. Their existence was unknown to numbers of Spanish-American landholders. Because of distance, Indian raids, and difficulties in transportation and communication, they were inaccessible to much of the Spanish-American territory. Moreover, the Anglo lawyers resident in urban centers and in communication with each other hovered over the land offices, quick to bribe officials and to take advantage of any unregistered land.

In a case in San Miguel County known to the writer, several Anglo lawyers active in politics around the turn of the century agreed to bring suit challenging the legality of a large community land grant. The villagers in panic requested one of the lawyers to defend their rights. As they had no money, they agreed to pay in land. The case wended its slow way through the courts until eventually the state supreme court decided in favor of the village. The lawyer took most of the better grazing land as fee and divided it up among the lawyers in the plot. Enormous amounts of land were alienated from Spanish-American ownership as payment for legal services. Many prominent Anglo lawyers refused to accept money for their services demanding that they be paid in land.

Because of violence and increasing land conflicts, a Court of Private Land Claims was established on July 1, 1891, and continued until June 30, 1904. The purpose of the court was to adjudicate land titles in New Mexico and Colorado originating in Spanish and Mexican land grants. The court consisted of five judges from other parts of the nation, a United States attorney, and other officials. All were Anglos and made their decisions upon the basis of Anglo law. The court rejected all land grant claims unless they measured up to the most rigorous requirements of Anglo procedures and conceptions of land ownership. Thus in this period, two-thirds of all Spanish-American land claims were rejected on the pretext of imperfect titles.

Many Spanish-Americans, caught in the web of a political and a judicial system that they found impossible to understand, frequently surrendered their lands without a struggle when their rights were challenged. Bitter, resentful, and unable to defend themselves, they shrank from all Anglo contacts. To them the entire legal process seemed like a giant Anglo conspiracy to steal their property without possibility of escape or redress.

Another aspect of the American political system imposed upon the Spanish-Americans that cost them staggering land losses was the American county system financed through property taxes. Ignorant of American political customs and unfamiliar with the land tax, the Spanish-Americans fell victim to the Anglo lawyers and businessmen and their Spanish-American allies who hovered over land tax records eagerly paying taxes on tax delinquent land. At times land taxes were juggled to sharply increase taxes until considerable land passed into Anglo ownership and then the taxes were reduced. In many counties the small irrigated parcels of the Spanish-Americans pay a much higher tax per acre than the large ranches of the Anglos even though the financial return is lower. Also in many counties, Spanish-Americans who did pay their land taxes were given fraudulent receipts or else the payments were not recorded in the tax records of the county. The situation became even more vicious in 1926 when the New Mexican state legislature passed a law that any land remaining tax delinquent for three years could be sold by the county. If a man paid up the delinquent taxes, the land became his.

With the coming of Anglo ranchers from Texas in the 1880s and 1890s, violence erupted all over New Mexico and southern Colorado. The unarmed Spanish-Americans with their traditions of peaceful community life came to regard the American cowboys as worse than the Comanches and Apaches. These ranchers treated the Spanish-Americans as though they were not human beings and had no rights that needed to be respected. They refused to accept them socially, dispossessed them of their lands, scattered their sheep, and drove off their cattle. The Spanish-Americans could only take refuge in a futile hate that has made the word Texan a hiss and a byword throughout northern New Mexico.

For example, in 1884, cowhands destroyed the home and ranch headquarters of Teofilo Trujillo, one of the earliest settlers of San Luis Valley, Colorado. Eventually they killed him. Lawless bands of Texans in Lincoln County, New Mexico, in 1864 rode through the county killing Spanish-Americans, driving many off their lands with the threat, sometimes fulfilled, of killing their wives and children. They also warned other Anglos against hiring Spanish-Americans. William A. Keleher states as follows:

> Many Texans will not allow a Mexican to be employed on any of the ranches in this part of the country, where by threat of violence they can prevent it; and they will go to all lengths and stop at nothing in the shape of perjury or misrepresentation to invalidate or to upset titles of Mexicans in the area.

Another technique used by Anglo ranchers and businessmen to obtain control and ownership of grant lands was to buy up land rights in a grant from a number of Spanish-American residents and then graze large herds of livestock on the grazing lands. When they became overgrazed and relatively useless to the small herds of the Spanish-Americans, the Anglo offered to buy up the grazing lands at a low price. If the Spanish-Americans refused to sell, the Anglo took the case to court and usually the judge ordered that the grant be dissolved, the lands sold, and proceeds distributed to the claimants. Many times, there was but one Anglo, by agreement, there to bid on the land. Many banks in Albuquerque financed such Anglo activities in the area.

There is evidence to indicate that one of the largest land grants in north central New Mexico and southern Colorado was lost through another interesting device. A very prominent Anglo lawyer and political figure in New Mexico noticed that no claim to the land grant had been filed in the

Santa Fe land office. He promptly filed claim and published intent in an English-speaking newspaper several hundred miles away on the other side of the Rocky Mountains. The local inhabitants knew nothing about it until many years later when Anglo ranchers began to fence in their lands. Then violence erupted that has continued until the present day.

The use of the fence has also been costly to the Spanish-Americans. Many Anglo ranchers fenced in large tracts of land. In eastern New Mexico entire villages were apt to be enclosed. Once the land was enclosed, intent of claim was also filed in English-speaking newspapers, seldom read by the Spanish-Americans. As the claims were not apt to be contested, the rancher obtained the land. The sheriff evicted the Spanish-Americans.

The various land activities of the federal government in New Mexico have caused the Spanish-Americans enormous land losses. Millions of acres of land traditionally used for grazing purposes in the valleys and mountains of northern New Mexico for many generations were lost when forest reserves were established and land granted to the railroads. The impact of this land loss is still felt in the northern villages in New Mexico.

Present forest administrators and forest rangers are apt to be Anglos and subconsciously or consciously biased against the Spanish-American and his numerous small herds of sheep and cattle in favor of the large Anglo commercial operator. The rangers even today are trying to persuade or to force the Spanish-Americans to leave the northern counties.

The homestead laws also caused tremendous land loss to the Spanish-Americans. Under these laws thousands of immigrants poured into New Mexico from Texas, Oklahoma, Arkansas, Iowa, and other states in the 1890s and 1900s. They settled on millions of acres used by the Spanish-Americans who had never registered title. As drought slowly squeezed out the homesteaders, the land passed into the hands of local Anglo merchants in payment of accounts or for cash. The merchants established large ranches or sold the land to incoming ranchers. Either way, the Spanish-Americans lost access to the land.

Anglo merchants also exploited the Spanish-Americans directly through their control of the local economy. They bought the Spanish-American products such as wool, lambs, and cattle at prices set by themselves. They encouraged the Spanish-Americans to use unlimited credit. At the end of a varying period of time, the merchant called for payment of the account. The Spanish-Americans, unable to pay, lost their land. This process is still at work in many northern New Mexico communities.

The construction of expensive reclamation, irrigation, and flood control projects in New Mexico brought about the introduction of a highly commercialized and partially subsidized agriculture that cost additional thousands of Spanish-Americans their land and water rights up and down the Rio Grande Valley. The imposition of heavy water or conservation charges upon land used for subsistence agriculture has brought about the replacement of Spanish-American by Anglo farmers around Albuquerque and in the Mesilla Valley around Las Cruces. This land loss still continues at the present time.

Oddly enough, the modern requirements of the New Mexico Department of Public Health is eroding away the limited land basis of many Spanish-American villages at the present time. Unable to secure public assistance if land is owned, many Spanish-Americans either abandon their land or sell it at whatever they can get and move to town and onto the public welfare roles.

Since 1854, the Spanish-Americans have lost over 2,000,000 acres of private lands, 1,700,000 acres of communal land, 1,800,000 acres taken by the state, and vast areas lost to the federal government. The impact of this enormous and continued land loss has been the collapse of the village economy, the growing sense of apathy and futility among the Spanish-American farmers, and an accelerated cultural break-down, juvenile delinquency, increase in family disorganiza-tion, continued and rapid rise of welfare roles, and an economic decline of the Spanish-American counties. Many of these counties are becoming depopulated as large num-bers move to cities in Colorado, California, and Arizona, transferring a complex social and economic problem from one state or county to another.

4

The So-Called Crime of Being a Wetback

Jorge A. Bustamante

Introduction

Those who illegally stream across the Mexico-United States border are called "wetbacks" because they cross the Rio Grande without the benefit of a bridge. All other illegal migrants from Mexico are referred to by the same term. Thus, wetback characterizes anyone who enters illegally from Mexico. The term, then, carries an unavoidable connotation —one who has broken the law. This paper will deal with some of the questions that arise from that connotation. In the first part, we describe the historical emergence of the wetback, discussing the roles of the persons involved in the violation of the immigration law and some of the socioeconomic consequences of the wetback as a deviant. In the second part, we examine the wetback as a case of deviance through labeling theory. In this approach the deviant character of the wetback is analyzed as a process of interaction. Each role in this process will be discussed in terms of its interests, power, and consequences with respect to those of the roles of the other participants. Finally, the concept of

This article originally appeared in the *American Journal of Sociology*, vol. 77, no. 4, under the title "The 'Wetback' as Deviant: An Application of Labeling Theory." Reprinted with permission.

"anti-law entrepreneur" is introduced, and its explanatory potential is indicated.

Historical Background

In 1882, during President Arthur's administration, the first immigration law was passed following a strong nativist movement. The same year the first "Chinese exclusion act" established significant limits to what was considered an "invasion of Orientals" who had been a preferred source of cheap labor for West Coast employers.[1] The search for cheap labor turned to Japanese and Filipino immigrants, who then became the target of "exclusionists." Campaigns like the "swat the Jap" campaign in Los Angeles and those inspired by the writings of Madison Lerant and Lothrop Stoddard led to further restrictions of immigration from the Orient. The "Asian barred zone" provisions excluded immigration from Oriental countries as a source for cheap labor.[2]

In the first decade of the century, eastern and southern European immigration became the focus of nativist and exclusionist crusades. Pressure generated by those movements crystallized in the appointment of a commission by the U.S. Congress to study immigration; the result of that study is known as the Dillingham Commission Report (1907–1910). Throughout this voluminous report a long-debated distinction between the "old" and "new" immigration was made. It was argued that the values and occupations of the "old immigrants" (Anglo-Saxons and Nordics) were threatened by the "newer immigrants," southern and eastern Europeans and Asians.[3] The distinction between new and old immigration created a dichotomy about which many pages of "scientific" reports were written in support of the undesirability of the new immigration.

Campaigns demanding restriction of the new immigration finally crystallized in the immigration laws of 1921 and 1924, which established quotas restricting immigration from all countries except those in the western hemisphere.

In the meantime, social scientists conducted research on the immigration phenomenon; they found empirical evidence showing that immigration to the United States has consistently supplied cheap labor.[4]

All countries which provided cheap labor for the United States were affected by the quota system established by the Immigration Act of 1921. Thus, the search for cheap labor turned to the western hemisphere, to which the quota system did not apply;[5] Mexican immigrants were found to be the most suitable replacement.[6] The suitability of Mexican labor rested on (1) geographical proximity; (2) the uninterrupted tradition of immigration, which was internal when most of southwestern United States was still part of Mexico;[7] and (3) unemployment and unrest in Mexico, created by several years of revolution.[8]

A tremendous increase in Mexican immigration during the first quarter of the century[9] corresponded to the increased demand for unskilled labor in the economic expansion of the Southwest. Mexicans crossed 1,870 miles of an almost completely open border[10] to reach the steel industry in East Chicago,[11] railroad construction, and, most significantly, agricultural expansion in the Southwest.[12]

In this period the Mexican who wanted to legally cross the border had to go through a complicated procedure to be admitted into the United States. Those procedures included, in particular, a literacy test, "a condition which many immigrants cannot fulfill."[13] Therefore, many took advantage of the "open" border policy toward Mexican laborers.

Moreover, the illegal immigrant could stay in the United States untroubled as long as he avoided the authorities who might disclose his status. Since no specific authorities were entrusted with apprehending illegal immigrants, the dangers of being caught were further minimized.[14] Thus the illegal immigrant's status was not visibly distinct from the legal immigrant's. The illegal entrant was able to maintain his violation in a state of "primary deviance." [15]

The appearance of the Border Patrol in 1924 altered the primary deviance of the illegal entrant by crystallizing a new social reaction to the violation of immigration laws. The new police force was to reveal those primary deviants, violators of immigration laws. In this process, the term "wetback," previously purely descriptive, acquired a new meaning. It became the "label" or "stigma" by which the illegal immigrant was made visible. At the same time, the label "wetback" also became the symbol by which the illegal immigrant was able to identify a new "me" for himself,[16] and a new role which better equipped him to meet the social reaction to his behavior (illegal entrance).[17]

The establishment of the Border Patrol in 1924 not only made the wetback more visible as a lawbreaker; it also brought changes in the patterns of behavior of the illegal immigrants. The freedom of interaction the illegal immigrant had had before 1924 was considerably reduced. He now had to walk, to speak, and to bear any treatment with the fear of being caught by or "turned in" to the Border Patrol.

The interaction most significantly changed was between illegal migrant worker and employer. Before 1924 labor conditions resulted from differential access to mechanisms of power and from the interplay of labor-force supply and demand. The organization of the Border Patrol brought a new factor: the illegal migrant could always be caught and sent back to Mexico. To be "turned in" became a threat always present in the migrant's mind that interfered with his social contacts. Social contacts, except for those with an employer or prospective employer, could be avoided for self-protection. The explicit or implicit threat of being denounced by the employer became a new significant element in the settlement of work contracts. It could be used to impose oppressive salaries and working conditions. In his search for a job he could no longer freely accept or reject a given offer; he always had to consider the alternative of being denounced to the Border Patrol.[18]

The importance of the "wetback problem" gains further emphasis in its numerical proportions. Although no reliable statistics exist on the actual number of wetbacks who have entered the United States, an approximate idea can be inferred from the records of expatriated wetbacks. Records for the period 1930–1969 indicate that 7,486,470 apprehensions of wetbacks were made by the U.S. Immigration Authority.[19] The highest rates were concentrated in the decades 1941–1960, during which 5,953,210 expulsions of wetbacks were made. The size of the population involved clearly defines the importance of the problem.

When we look at the sociocultural characteristics of the persons involved, we see that the problem is much larger. Most are poor peasants from central and northern states in Mexico who come to the United States only to find work to survive.[20] They are willing to accept anything—good or bad treatment, illness, starvation, low wages, poor living conditions; all are taken philosophically and accepted without struggle. Their struggle is concentrated on pure survival.[21]

The Network of Social Relations of Wetbacks

Various groups of people come in contact with the wetback in the United States. In this section we will review four major groups: (1) the employer who benefits from a cheap labor pool, (2) the southwestern Mexican-American farmworker who suffers from the competition of these low-paid workers, (3) the lawmaker who is in the ambiguous position of defender of the law and protector of the "illegal" interests of farm entrepreneurs, and (4) the law enforcer who is directly responsible for enforcing the laws.

The Employer

In all economic enterprises, and in particular agricultural enterprises, labor constitutes a major segment of production costs. Rational manipulation of all instruments of production in pure economic terms requires the minimization of costs in all areas to achieve the highest possible economic return. Workers willing to accept labor contracts below going wages clearly become a positive asset in that they assure higher returns for the entrepreneur. Moreover, other economic advantages besides low wages accrue from the employment of wetback labor. First, in some kinds of employment no strict accounting of working hours is kept, since work contracts based on daily labor may involve as many as twelve hours.[22] Second, little or no responsibility for disability occurs, since the wetback must assume responsibility for his own injuries and accidents. Third, the employer is under no obligation, legal or otherwise, to provide health and medical services, sanitary facilities, or even decent housing.[23] As a result, what the wetback receives as wages and other standard "fringe benefits" is determined only by the employer's conscience and the current standards of neighbors and friends.[24] Even in pure economic terms, then, the position of the rural entrepreneur vis-à-vis the wetback is highly advantageous; by using wetbacks as workers, farmers can maximize possible economic gains in labor costs.[25]

The Mexican-American Farmworker

Whereas the rural entrepreneur gains by the presence of wetbacks, the Mexican-American rural workers lose in competition for jobs. They feel that wetbacks push work contract conditions to the lowest possible level, a "charity" level out of step with living requirements in the United States. Their personal suffering from such competition is unjust, since, while being penalized by this competition, they have to pay the costs of citizenship (e.g., income and other taxes) and receive little or no benefit from such required contributions. Further, wetbacks break the possible cohesion of the rural labor force, and so they lose bargaining power with rural entrepreneurs. Finally, the manipulation of the mass media and urban lobbying groups by the rural entrepreneur creates an artificial shortage of labor which serves to ensure the permanence of wetbacks. At the same time, Mexican-American workers are prevented from speaking in the mass media to unmask the artificial labor shortage.[26]

The Lawmaker

The lawmaker should be the one to bridge the gap between the conflicting demands of the entrepreneur and the Mexican-American. Nevertheless, the most general pattern followed by lawmakers is to consider the wetback problem and the working situation on the border as something unavoidable or expected. Legal attempts to effectively prevent the wetback from crossing the border are stricken from proposed codes by the lawmakers on the rationale that the farmer along the border wants wetback labor.[27] The "realistic" attitude of these lawmakers seems to be either that it is convenient to conform to or worthless to struggle against the situation. Thus, the U.S. immigration law is broken in order to maintain a supply of wetbacks. For many southern, and in particular Texas, legislators, there is no evil in maintaining the influx of wetbacks.

Protection of the interests of wetback employers by lawmakers is best illustrated by a law (U.S. Congress, 8 U.S.C., section 1324, 1952) which makes it a felony to be a wetback but not to hire one.[28] This is a paradoxical situation which legitimizes the hiring of wetbacks in spite of the general recognition that it is the possibility of being hired that attracts Mexican workers to cross illegally to the United States. This situation was pointed out by Ruben Salazar (recently killed in the Chicano Moratorium in Los Angeles) in an article published in the *Los Angeles Times* of April 27, 1970: "There is no law against hiring wetbacks. There is only a law against being a wetback." [29]

The Law Enforcer

The Border Patrol is directly responsible for the prevention of wetback crossings and for the apprehension of wetbacks already in the United States. Theoretically, such a role would place the patrol in direct confrontation with the rural entrepreneurs using wetback labor, inasmuch as they enforce laws made in the interests of the total society. Their activities would, in part, protect the immediate interests of the legal rural workers.

Nevertheless, evidence suggests that such relationships of reciprocity are not realized; instead, the conflict between the Border Patrol and entrepreneurs is somehow transformed into covert cooperation through a "pattern of evasion" of the law.[30] This transformation involves the following: First, the entrepreneurs offer little resistance to the apprehension of wetbacks, in exchange for the patrol's overlooking the wetbacks when work needs to be done. Second, wetbacks openly at work may informally legitimate their status as workers and thus remain unharassed. Third, complete enforcement of the law by state and national authorities, and with minimum cooperation from local people, is theoretically possible.[31]

The Labeling Approach to Deviant Behavior

Theories which view deviance as a quality of the deviant act or the actor cannot help us understand the wetback as deviant. "Wetback" became the label for a deviant after the appearance of the Border Patrol, and various social groups came to *react* differently to the presence of wetbacks. It is singularly characteristic of this deviant type that it occurs in a cross-cultural context; as a Mexican, the wetback breaks an American law and receives negative legal sanction while, at the same time, he positively fulfills the needs of specific American groups. This context of deviance fits well into the framework of labeling theory. According to Howard Becker, deviance cannot be viewed as homogeneous because it results from interaction and consists of particular responses by various social groups to a particular behavior of the prospective deviant or outsider.[32]

In this context, we must analyze the wetback in interaction, singling out the responses of the various groups making up the network which labels his behavior as deviant. The deviant character of the wetback, then, lies not in him nor in his behavior but in the superimposition of the deviant label on him.

Becker's use of labeling theory in deviance is of particular interest to us because of his stress on the political dimensions of the labeling processes. He emphasizes the fact that the legal norms and the behavior classified as deviant must be viewed as part of a political process in which group A, *in conflict* with group B, defines the rules for group B. The degree of group A's success in imposing such rules and in enforcing them depends primarily upon the political and economic power of group A. Furthermore, the will of group A is often an expression of a class interest rather than solely of individual members of group A. In such a case, enforcement of the rules becomes applicable to all members of that class, excluding members of group B whose class interests are the same as group A's.

Becker further indicates that labeling always begins with the initiative of a "moral entrepreneur," a leader (individual or group) who crusades for new rules to stop something that he views as wrong. Moral entrepreneurs are interested in the content of rules and are very often involved in what they view as humanitarian or moral reformism. In their crusades, they typically say they want to help those beneath them to achieve a better status, and in the process "they add to the power they derive from the legitimacy of their moral position the power they derive from their superior position in society." [33] The outcome of a successful moral crusade is the establishment of a new set of rules (i.e., the immigration laws of 1921 and 1924) and corresponding enforcement agencies and officials (i.e., the U.S. Border Patrol). The new law enforcers justify their existence by attempting to fulfill the new activities, and, in their performance, they try to win the respect of prominent persons.

Once a law and its enforcers come into existence the process of labeling becomes independent of the moral entrepreneur. The enforcer becomes the most important actor, and while enforcing the law he stigmatizes or labels certain individuals as deviants. Thus, there is a process of interaction in which some actors will enforce rules "in the service of their own interest," whereas others, also "in the service of their own interest," commit acts labeled as deviant.[34]

The Wetback Labeling Process

The labeling process started with a moral crusade under the leadership of moral entrepreneurs representing the moral spirit of the American legal system. The results of the crusade were new legal codes (the immigration laws of 1921 and 1924) and the establishment of organizations and specialized personnel (e.g., the Border Patrol) to implement the new codes. The moral component of the legitimization of the new codes rests on the righteousness of the law, inasmuch as it protects the interests of nationals who otherwise would be defenseless against the threat of foreign competitors.

This organizational superstructure, whose purpose was to carry out the moral imperatives, resulted in a radical transformation of the previous interactions of foreign laborers. Of immediate concern was the reinforcement of the illegal status of immigrant workers under the deviant label of wetback. Nevertheless, moral imperatives, even those incorporated legally and implemented by specialized personnel, are not the only basis of motivation and rationalization of action. Others, especially political and economic interests, can be at variance with these new moral imperatives and influence behavior. When we examine such conflicting motivations we see that they may be selectively used, depending on the context of the action and the character of the actor—in particular his power. Thus, the rural entrepreneur in certain situations (e.g., harvest time) uses economic motivation to hire wetbacks with contracts calling for long hours of work and the lowest possible pay. In other situations (say, when he has unwanted workers) he uses the moral imperative to denounce wetbacks to the Border Patrol. A similar differential use of motivation occurs with other groups. It is necessary to specify the nature of motivations at play in the wetback case.

Looking at interests as a source of motivations, we shall focus on them at the juncture where they shape action; that is, at the point of interaction between wetbacks and the groups of actors discussed in this paper. A distinction will be made between group interests related to the presence of the wetback and group interests related only to each actor's role independent of the presence of the wetback. The latter would be those interests pertaining to the maintenance of the role played by actors of each group, that is, (1) the Mexican-American farmworker's role interest would be to maximize wages, (2) the farmer's (wetback employer's) role interest would be to maximize profit, (3) the lawmaker's role interest would be to provide legislation that meets the necessities of his constituencies and the country, (4) the law enforcer's (Border Patrol's) role interest would be to enforce immigration laws, (5) the moral entrepreneur's role interest would be to define good and evil for society. On the other hand, group interest related to the presence of the wetback seems to indicate a different dimension of each actor's role, as, respectively, (1) to stop the influx of wetbacks in order to avoid their competition for jobs and to increase bargaining power vis-à-vis the farmer, (2) to maximize profits by the use of the wetback cheap labor, (3) to gain political support from the farmers by protecting their interests, (4) to enforce immigration laws selectively, (5) to define protection of nationals against foreign competition as good and entrance to the United States without inspection as immoral.

This distinction of interests seems to promote understanding of some contradictions in the wetback phenomenon, such as (1) condemning the wetback by defining him as a deviant and, at the same time, maintaining a demand for his labor force which is reflected in a steadily increasing influx of wetbacks each year;[35] (2) penalizing a person for being a wetback, but not a farmer for hiring one; (3) maintaining an agency for the enforcement of immigration laws and at the same time exerting budget limitations and/or political pressures to prevent successful enforcement of the law.[36]

These are some of the contradictions that become apparent in the wetback case, but they are nothing less than reflections of contradictions in society at large. This is particularly obvious to us when we see the conflict of interests between the farmer and Mexican-American farmworker (each tries to maximize his economical gains at the expense of the other) and when we see the presence of the wetback kept undercover as a veil hiding deeper conflict. Indeed, when the role of the wetback is introduced in agricultural production, we see a different conflict of interests taking place—namely, that between the Mexican-American worker and the wetback. The former blames the latter for lowering working conditions and standards of living.

The nature of the two conflicts should be differentiated. Whereas the conflict of interests between the Mexican-American farmworker and the farmer is determined by the position each plays in a particular mode of agricultural production, the conflict between the Mexican-American worker and the wetback is determined primarily by a set of beliefs that are not necessarily grounded in reality, namely, that wages and working conditions are determined by external laws of supply and demand independent of the employers; that the wetback *causes* low wages and low standards of living for the farmworker, etc. It is important to note the point here that the conflicts "created" by the wetback would disappear with an unrestricted enforcement of immigration laws.

Another aspect of our discussion of group interest is the power that supports each specified interest and respective action. Since the groups themselves reflect status differentials, it is the differences in power (and possible collisions of power) that give form to the interaction. Furthermore, the power legitimization of these actions sustains the existing form against any possible transformation.

Power differences among the various actors result from their ability to manipulate or influence interaction in the direction of their interests.[37] In this interpretation, the wetback employer is clearly the most powerful category, since he is able to influence all other actors. On the other extreme is the wetback. He clearly appears at a disadvantage. As an outsider he has no legitimacy. He is not eligible for public assistance or for the benefits of an eventual "moral entrepreneur," since he is not eligible to stay in the country, unless he is in jail. He is also not eligible for other benefits because of the stigma of having once broken the immigration laws. This might, technically, prevent him from acquiring legal residence or citizenship in the United States. The wetback only has the original motivation which made him cross the border (survival) and a new one resulting from the deviant label (not to be caught) which becomes another element of pure survival. As an outsider with such elemental interests he dares not complain—the only possible protest comes when his survival is in jeopardy and his only course of action is to return to Mexico.

A Conceptual Addendum to Becker's Schema

Labeling theory provides us with the concept of moral entrepreneur. Applying the elements of this type to the case under analysis, we find a new type in the role of the wetback employer. His crusade is directed toward the self-serving enforcement of existing laws. The source of his crusade is the threat of the loss of cheap labor that would occur if the laws were enforced. Evidently the characteristics of this second type are the polar opposites of those of the moral entrepreneur. The imperative he singles out as a banner is economic rather than moral. The crusade he leads is supported by power and economic interest rather than moral righteousness. This type can perhaps be characterized as an *antilaw entrepreneur*. In order to be successful he associates the law enforcer and the lawmaker in his enterprise and becomes able to manipulate the law in two ways: first, by preventing its enforcement whenever he needs cheap labor; second, by stimulating its enforcement when he needs to dispose of a complaining or useless wetback.

A view of the contradictions of society apparent in the wetback case has allowed us to introduce the antilaw entrepreneur. Such a concept is useful for the understanding of deviance because it shows that violation of a law can also become the goal of an enterprise in the same sense that the creation of a law may be the goal of an enterprise. Both crusades, to be successful, require leaders holding legitimate power, although in one case they have the added legitimization of answering to a moral imperative, whereas in the other they answer to the economic interests of a specialized group. The law enforcer, the lawmaker, and a powerful group of rural entrepreneurs can launch such a crusade against the law and yet not be "labeled" as deviants.

If a Border Patrol man states firmly that to enforce the law would "ruin the fields," [38] and a lawmaker refers to specific measures in the Senate to allow the influx of wetbacks,[39] and a former vice-president of the United States (John Nance Garner) says, "If they [wetback employers] get the Mexican labor it enables them to make a profit," [40] then the essential objectives of the enterprise are spelled out. The continuing presence of wetbacks is in no little measure an indication of the success of the antilaw entrepreneur.

Conclusion

The preceding analysis leads us to see:

1. The wetback as one who crosses the U.S.-Mexican border illegally, taking advantage of the limited enforcement of the U.S. immigration laws.

2. The interaction process in which such a man is labeled as deviant, a label that will constitute a central element of a process of exploitation.

3. The deviant label making the wetback more attractive as a worker than the Mexican-American (at the same time, paradoxically, such a label—an element of destitution—becomes what the wetback exchanges for an unstable taste of survival).

4. The labeling process in which the wetback is "created," in which interests and power are arranged in an action that we have typified as an antilaw enterprise.

And finally, we see a human being with the alternatives of being exploited by a country forcing him to become a deviant or of facing misery in his own country by not doing so.

Notes

1. Carl Wittke, "Immigration Policy Prior to World War I," in *The Annals,* ed. Thorston Sellin (Philadelphia: American Academy of Political and Social Science, 1949), p. 13.
2. Roger Daniels and Harry Kitano, *American Racism: Exploration of the Nature of Prejudice* (Englewood Cliffs, N.J.: Prentice-Hall, 1970), p. 53.

3. Isaac A. Hourwich, *Immigration and Labor* (New York: G. P. Putnam, 1912) p. 19.

4. Ibid., pp. 167–172; Ross A. Eckler and Jack Zlotnick, "Immigration and Labor Force," in *The Annals*, ed. Thorston Sellin.

5. Charles F. Mandan and Gladys Meyer, *Minorities in American Society* (New York: American Book Co., 1968), p. 104.

6. Julian Samora and Jorge A. Bustamante, "Mexican Immigration and American Labor Demands," in *Migrant and Seasonal Farmworkers' Powerlessness.* Hearings, U. S. Senate Committee on Labor and Public Welfare, Pt. 7 (Washington, D.C.: Government Printing Office, 1971).

7. Carey McWilliams, *North from Mexico* (1948; reprint ed., Westport, Conn.: Greenwood Press, 1968), pp. 162–169.

8. Jorge A. Bustamante, *Don Chano: Autobiografía de un Emigrante Méxicano* (Mexico: Institute of Social Investigation, University of Mexico, in press).

9. Leo Grebler, *Mexican Immigration to the United States*, Report #2 (Los Angeles: Mexican-American Study Project, 1966), p. 20.

10. Manuel Gamio, *Mexican Immigration to the United States* (Chicago: University of Chicago Press, 1930), p. 10.

11. Julian Samora and Richard Lamanna, "Mexican-American in a Midwest Metropolis: A Study of East Chicago," in *The Mexican-American People: The Nation's Second Largest Minority*, ed. V. Webb (New York: Free Press, 1970).

12. Julian Samora, assisted by J. A. Bustamante and G. Cardenas, *Los Mojados, the Wetback Story* (Notre Dame, Ind.: University of Notre Dame Press, 1971).

13. Gamio, *Mexican Immigration*, p. 11.

14. Lamar B. Jones, "Mexican American Labor Problems in Texas." Ph.D. diss., University of Texas, 1965, p. 13.

15. Edwin M. Lemert, *Social Pathology* (New York: McGraw-Hill, 1951).

16. George H. Mead, "The Psychology of Punitive Justice," in *American Journal of Sociology* 23 (March 1918), pp. 577–602.

17. Edwin M. Lemert, *Human Deviance, Social Problems, and Social Control* (Englewood Cliffs, N.J.: Prentice-Hall, 1967), pp. 42–51.

18. Data from 493 interviews that I conducted with wetbacks in

1969 show that 8 percent of the interviewees were "turned in" by their employers without being paid for their work. A year later, similar situations were encountered by the author during a participant observation as a "wetback" conceived to validate previous findings. A report of these experiences and the larger research project appears in Samora, *Los Mojados,* and further evidence of these and other kinds of exploitation of the "wetback" are reported by Lyle Saunders and Olen F. Leonard, *The Wetback in the Lower Rio Grande Valley of Texas* (Austin, Tex.: University of Texas Inter-American Educational Occasional Papers, 1951), 7, p. 72; Eleanor M. Hadley, "A Critical Analysis of the Wetback Problem," in *Law and Contemproary Problems* 21 (Spring 1956), p. 352; and Jones, "Mexican American Labor Problems," pp. 14–22.

19. U.S. Immigration and Naturalization Service, *Annual Report* (Washington, D.C.: Government Printing Office, 1966), and *Report of Field Operations 1967–68.*

20. Samora, *Los Mojados,* p. 102.

21. Saunders and Leonard, *The Wetback in the Lower Rio Grande Valley,* p. 6.

22. Hadley, "A Critical Analysis," p. 347.

23. American G.I. Forum of Texas and Texas State Federation of Labor, *What Price Wetbacks?* (Austin, Tex.: AFL, 1953), pp. 17–27.

24. Hadley, "A Critical Analysis," p. 347.

25. Samora, *Los Mojados,* pp. 98–103.

26. Hadley, "A Critical Analysis," p. 345.

27. U.S. Congress, Senate, Appropriation Hearings on S.1917 before the Committee of the Judiciary subcommittee, 83rd Cong., 1st sess., 1953, p. 10.

28. That law provides that "any person who willfully or knowingly conceals, harbors, or shields from detection, in any place including any building or by any means of transportation, or who encourages or induces, or attempts to encourage or induce, either directly or indirectly, the entry into the United States of any alien shall be guilty of a felony. Upon conviction he shall be punished by a fine not exceeding $2,000 or by imprisonment for a term not exceeding five years, or both, for each alien in respect to whom the violation occurs. Provided,

however, that for the purposes of this section, employment, including the usual and normal practices incident to employment, shall not be deemed to constitute harboring." (Samora, *Los Mojados*, p. 139.)

29. Ibid., p. 139.
30. Saunders and Leonard, *The Wetback in the Lower Rio Grande Valley*, p. 68; Robin Williams, Jr., *American Society: A Sociological Interpretation* (New York: Knopf, 1951).
31. Saunders and Leonard, *The Wetback in the Lower Rio Grande Valley*, p. 68.
32. Howard S. Becker, *Outsiders. Studies in the Sociology of Deviance* (New York: Free Press, 1963), p. 91.
33. Ibid., pp. 147–163.
34. Ibid., p. 162.
35. Samora, *Los Mojados*, pp. 195–196.
36. Hadley, "A Critical Analysis," p. 348.
37. William Gamson, *Power and Discontent* (Homewood, Ill.: Dorsey, 1968).
38. Saunders and Leonard, *The Wetback in the Lower Rio Grande Valley*, p. 68.
39. Senate Appropriation Hearings on S.1917. (Senator McCarran)
40. Jones, "Mexican American Labor Problems," p. 17.

5

I Am My Brother
in the Same Struggle for Justice
Manuel Gómez

Chicano resistance to the U.S. war in Indochina and to the draft has grown strong in recent years. Chicanos know that they are being drafted and dying in numbers far out of proportion to their percentage of the population. They have also come to realize that their real enemy is not the people of Indochina but the system that oppresses them here at home, that the Vietnamese and others are in fact their brothers in a common struggle. The following letter, which appeared in El Grito del Norte *on March 28, 1970, is one expression of these feelings.*

Today, December 8, 1969, I must refuse induction into the Armed Services of the United States. Please understand it is difficult for me to communicate my feelings through writing, but nevertheless I will try to let you see through my window.

In my veins runs the blood of all the people of all the world. I am a son of La Raza, the universal children, and cannot be trained and ordered to kill my brother. When the first man was killed, too many had died. For my people, I refuse to respect your induction papers.

It is well known that Mexicans were among the first victims of your empire. The memory of the Mexican-American War is still an open wound in the souls of my people.

140

The Treaty of Guadalupe Hidalgo is a lie, similar to all the treaties signed with our Indian brothers. The war did not end. It has continued in the minds and hearts of the people of the Southwest. Strife and bloodshed have never stopped between us. This society with its Texas Rangers and Green Berets has never allowed our people to live in peace. The blood is still moist on the land. Too many of my brothers have died fighting for a lie called "American Freedom," both in our streets and in foreign lands.

My people have known nothing but racist tyranny and brutal oppression from this society. Your educational system has butchered our minds, stung our hearts, and poisoned our souls. You cut out our tongues and castrated our culture, making us strangers in our own land. The sweat of my people watered the fields and their aching bones harvested your food. Today we continue to do your sweat work for you, with our hands and backs. Though you occupy the land, you have not conquered us. I am a free man. I choose my own battles. My fight is here.

In the short time you have held the land we have felt the pain of seeing beautiful lands turn into parking lots and freeways, of seeing the birds disappear, the fish die, and the waters become undrinkable, seeing the sign "Private Property" hung on a fence surrounding lands once held in common, and having our mountains become but vague shadows behind a veil of choking smog.

Your judges armed with the cold sword called Law, held in the diseased arm of Justice, have frozen the life of my brothers in your barbaric prisons, scarring them deeply. A man steals to live and you call him a criminal and lock him up worse than an animal. A soldier massacres and pillages a village, and he's made a hero, awarded a medal. I believe that if it is wrong to kill within society, then it must also be wrong to kill outside of the society. I am of a peace-loving people.

I see rabid leaders of this land live in luxury and comfort while they send my poor brothers to kill in a war no one wants to understand. The helpless and the innocent have lost on both sides as has been the case in all wars. My ears hear the scream of the fatherless children, my head hurts with the tears of mothers moaning for their sons, my soul shrinks from the knowledge of the unspeakable horrors of Song My and the rest to come. For the Vietnamese people, I refuse to respect your induction papers.

I cannot betray the blood of my brothers. We are all branches of the same tree, flowers of the same garden, waves of the same sea. The Vietnamese people are not my enemy, but brothers involved in the same struggle for justice against a common enemy. We are all under the same sky. East and West are one.

My heart is dedicated to seeking justice and peace in this world. My eyes see a new sun, with a far more beautiful horizon, where all the trees can see the sky and share the same water from the one river. I cannot fight for the enemy of the spirit of life. For my soul, I refuse to obey your induction orders.

PEACE AND JUSTICE,
Manuel Gómez
Temescal, Califas
Aztlán

6

Notes on Chicano Theater

Luis Váldez

Luis Váldez founded the Teatro Campesino in the early days of the grape strike, as a bilingual theater in which Chicano farmworkers were the actors and their experiences were the subject matter. He has continued to work with Chicanos in the teatro and also continues to write plays, essays, and so forth. Chicano theater has a long tradition, with roots in both the Spanish and Indian past. Today it forms part of the great cultural renaissance which is a vital part of the Chicano movement.

What is Chicano theater? It is theater as beautiful, *rasquachi*, human, cosmic, broad, deep, tragic, comic, as the life of La Raza itself. At its high point Chicano theater is religion—the *huelgistas* of Delano praying at the shrine of the Virgin of Guadalupe, located in the rear of an old station wagon parked across the road from Di Giorgios' camp 4; at its low point, it is a *cuento* or a *chiste* told somewhere in the recesses of the barrio, *puro pedo*.

Chicano theater, then, is first a reaffirmation of LIFE. That is what all theater is supposed to do, of course, but the

This essay originally appeared in *El Teatro*, Summer 1970, and is reprinted with permission.

limp, superficial, *gringo seco* productions in the "pro-fessional" American theater (and the college and university drama departments that serve it) are so antiseptic, they are antibiotic (antilife). The characters and life situations emerging from our little teatros are too real, too full of *sudor, sangre,* and body smells to be boxed in. Audience participation is no cute production trick with us; it is a preestablished, preassumed privilege. *Que le suenen la campanita!*

Defining Chicano theater is a little like defining a Chicano car. We can start with a low-rider's cool Merc or a campesino's banged-up Chevy, and describe the various paint jobs, hub caps, dents, taped windows, Virgins on the dashboard, etc. that define the car as particularly Raza. Underneath all the trimmings, however, is an unmistakable production of Detroit, an extension of General Motors. Consider now a theater that uses the basic form, the vehicle, created by Broadway or Hollywood: that is, the "realistic" play. Actually, this type of play was created in Europe, but where French, German, and Scandinavian playwrights went beyond realism and naturalism long ago, commercial gaba-cho theater refuses to let go.

It reflects a characteristic "American" hang-up on the material aspect of human existence. European theater, by contrast, has been influenced since around 1900 by the unrealistic, formal rituals of Oriental theater.

What do Oriental and European theater have to do with teatros Chicanos? Nothing, except that we are talking about a theater that is particularly our own, not another imitation of the gabacho. If we consider our origins, say the theater of the Mayans or the Aztecs, we are talking about something totally unlike the realistic play and more Chinese or Japanese in spirit. Kabuki, as a matter of fact, started long ago as something like our *actos* and evolved over two centuries into the highly exacting art form it is today; but it still contains *pleberias.* It evolved from and still belongs to *el pueblo japonés.*

In Mexico, before the coming of the white man, the greatest examples of total theater were, of course, the human sacrifices. *El Rabinal Achi*, one of the few surviving pieces of indigenous theater, describes the sacrifice of a courageous *guerrillero*, who, rather than dying passively on the block, is granted the opportunity to fight until he is killed. It is a tragedy naturally, but it is all the more transcendent because of the *guerrillero*'s identification, through sacrifice, with God. The only "set" such a drama-ritual needed was a stone-block; nature took care of the rest.

But since the Conquest, Mexico's theater, like its society, has had to imitate Europe and, in recent times, the United States. In this same vein, Chicanos in Spanish classes are frequently involved in productions of plays by Lope de Vega, Calderón de la Barca, Tirso de Molina, and other classic playwrights. Nothing is wrong with this, but it does obscure the Indio fountains of Chicano culture. Is Chicano theater, in turn, to be nothing but an imitation of gabacho playwrights, with barrio productions of racist works by Eugene O'Neill and Tennessee Williams? Will Broadway produce a Chicano version of *Hello, Dolly* now that it has produced a Black one?

The nature of Chicanismo calls for a revolutionary turn in the arts as well as in society. Chicano theater must be revolutionary in technique as well as content. It must be popular, subject to no other critics except the pueblo itself, but it must also educate the pueblo toward an appreciation of *social change*, on and off the stage.

It is particularly important for teatro Chicano to draw a distinction between what is theater and what is reality. A demonstration with a thousand Chicanos, all carrying flags and picket signs, shouting CHICANO POWER! is not the revolution. It is theater about the revolution. The people must act in *reality*, not on stage (which could be anywhere, even a sidewalk), in order to achieve real change. La Raza gets excited, *simon*, but unless the demonstration evolves into a street battle (which has not yet happened but is possible) it is basically a lot of emotion with very little political power, as Chicanos have discovered by demonstrating, picketing, and shouting before school boards, police departments, and stores, to no avail.

Such guerrilla theater passing as a demonstration has its uses, of course. It is agit-prop theater, as the gabachos used to call it in the 1930s: agitation and propaganda. It helps to stimulate and sustain the mass strength of a crowd. Hitler was very effective with this kind of theater, from the swastika to the Wagneresque stadium at Nuremberg. On the other end of the political spectrum, the Huelga march to Sacramento in 1966 was pure guerrilla theater. The red and black thunderbird flags of the United Farmworkers' Organizing Committee (UFWOC) (then the National Farmworkers' Association) and the standard of the Virgin of Guadalupe challenged the bleak sterility of Highway 99. Its emotional impact was irrefutable. Its actual political power was somewhat less.

But beyond the mass struggle of La Raza in the fields and barrios of America, there is an internal struggle in the very *corazón* of our people. That struggle, too, calls for revolutionary change. Our belief in God, the Church, the social role of women—these must be subject to examination and redefining in some kind of public forum. And that again means teatro. Not a teatro composed of *actos* or agit-prop but a teatro of ritual, of music, of beauty and spiritual sensitivity. A teatro of legends and myths. A teatro of religious strength. This type of theater will require real dedication; it may, indeed, require a couple of generations of Chicanos devoted to the use of the theater as an instrument in the evolution of our people.

The teatros in existence today reflect the most intimate understanding of everyday events in the barrios from which they have emerged. But, if Aztlán is to become reality, then we as Chicanos must not be reluctant to act nationally—to think in national terms, politically, economically, and spiritually. We must destroy the deadly regionalism that keeps us apart. The concept of a national theater for La Raza is intimately related to our evolving nationalism in Aztlán.

Consider a Teatro Nacional de Aztlán that performs with the same skill and prestige as the Ballet Folklórico de México (not for gabachos, however, but for La Raza). Such a teatro could carry the message of La Raza into Latin America, Europe, Japan, Africa—in short, all over the world. It would draw its strength from all the small teatros in the barrios, in terms of people and their plays, songs, designs; and it would give back funds, training, and augmented strength of national unity. One season the teatro members would be on tour with the Teatro Nacional; the next season they would be back in the barrio sharing their skills and experience. It would accommodate about 150 people altogether, with twenty to twenty-five in the Nacional and the rest spread out in various parts of Aztlán, working with the campesino, the urbano, the mestizo, the *piojo*, etc.

Above all, the national organization of teatros Chicanos would be self-supporting and independent, meaning no government grants. The *corazón* of La Raza cannot be revolutionalized on a grant from Uncle Sam. Though many of the teatros, including El Campesino, have been born out of preestablished political groups—thus making them harbingers of that particular group's viewpoint, news, and political prejudices—there is yet a need for independence for the following reasons: objectivity, artistic competence, survival. El Teatro Campesino was born in the Huelga, but the very Huelga would have killed it, if we had not moved sixty miles to the north of Delano. A struggle like the Huelga needs every person it can get to serve its immediate goals in order to survive; the Teatro, as well as the clinic, service center, and newspaper, being less important at the moment of need than the survival of the Union, were always losing people to the grape boycott. When it became clear to us that the

UFWOC would succeed and continue to grow, we felt it was time for us to move and to begin speaking out about things beyond the Huelga: Vietnam, the barrio, racial discrimination, etc.

The teatros must never get away from La Raza. Without the *palomia* sitting there, laughing, crying, and sharing whatever is on the stage, the teatros will dry up and die. If La Raza will not come to theater, then the theater must go to La Raza. This, in the long run, will determine the shape, style, content, spirit, and form of el teatro Chicano.

Pachucos, campesinos, low-riders, *pintos, chavalonas, familias, cuñados, tíos, primos*, Mexican-Americans, all the human essence of the barrio is starting to appear in the mirror of our theater. With them come the joys, sufferings, disappointments, and aspirations of our *gente*. We challenge Chicanos to become involved in the art, the life style, the political and religious act of doing theater.

7

Statement
of the Revolutionary Caucus
(Chicano Youth Liberation
Conference, 1969)

In March 1969 some 3,000 young Chicanos gathered at the Crusade for Justice in Denver, Colorado, to hold the first national Chicano Youth Conference, at which El Plan Espiritual de Aztlán was adopted. The statement of the "revolutionary caucus" also came out of that conference.

We, a nonconquered people living in a conquered land, come together hoping that a plan of liberation, a concrete revolutionary program acceptable to the entire Southwest, will come from this conference. Subjected to a system that has denied our human dignity, our rights are also being denied under a constitution which we had no part in formulating and, more fundamentally, the rights protected under the Treaty of Guadalupe Hidalgo which grants the right to cultural autonomy have been violated.

For 144 years we have been trying to peacefully coexist but no peace has come to our communities. Revolution is the only means available to us. We owe no allegiance, no respect, to any of the laws of this racist country. Our liberation struggle is a war of survival.

To us, nationalism is an awareness that we are not Caucasian, not Mexican-American or any other label the system puts upon us, but that we are a people with an ancient heritage and an ancient scar on our souls. Because we know who we are, our nationalism becomes an internationalism that does not deny the human dignity of any other people, but accepts them as brothers.

Our culture has been castrated through the various institutions of this system. We have known the profound pain of becoming strangers in our own land, of seeing beautiful lands turned into parking lots, of seeing birds disappear and fish die and waters become undrinkable, and the sign "private property" hung on a fence around land that once was held in common, of mountains becoming but vague shadows to our lives behind a veil of smog. We are being killed in Vietnam yet our lands are in the hands of strangers.

Can we attain control of our lives and liberate our people under the present system? Before we can answer this we must be aware of how this racist system oppresses us. We are oppressed first because we are Chicanos, because our skin is dark. But we are also exploited as workers by a system which feeds like a vulture off the work of our people only to enrich a few who own and control this entire country. We suffer a double oppression. We catch double hell.

But its oppression is not limited to us. It is a world system of oppression responsible for the misery of the mass of humanity. We will not attain what is rightfully ours, or our democratic right of self-determination, without having to overturn the entire system. We will have to do away with our oppressor's entire system of exploitation. In order to do this we must build a revolutionary organization which will fight on all levels to improve our conditions here and now, while at the same time seeing the longer range struggle which will definitively end racist society, exploitation, and guarantee our rights.

We make a call to all Mexicanos to put aside our so-called

regional differences and realize our similarities: the greatest ones being that we do have a basic common experience of exploitation, and a common enemy that must be destroyed before we can be a free people, masters of our lives.

8

La Raza Unida Party in the Chicano Movement

Jorge A. Bustamante
and
Gilberto López y Rivas

La Raza Unida Party is considered one of the most important developments in the Chicano movement; many Chicanos believe it can unify La Raza. The following article, written in early 1973, discusses the significance of La Raza Unida.

> *If the dogs bark*
> *it's that we are on our way*
> —Popular Spanish saying

The present stage of the Chicano people's struggle began only a short time ago, yet very important changes have already taken place in the fields of both ideology and organization. The emergence of La Raza Unida Party is at present the definitive event in this process of change.

Before La Raza Unida Party was established, one of the main characteristics of the different Chicano organizing efforts was their regional limitations. Often this problem resulted from the very nature of the organizations; sometimes it was the result of severe repression experienced by the more effective or radical groups; and many times it resulted from a general absence of the objective and subjective conditions necessary for the creation of an organization that could unify Chicano political efforts on a national scale.

Thus, in terms of goals as well as membership and political effectiveness, Chicano movement groups could not move beyond their particular orientation—which was either local or limited to certain specific problems. As a result, Chicano organizations before La Raza Unida Party were unable to offer a political framework which embraced all the problems of the Chicano people, which provided the necessary organizational structure and tactics, and which could win the support and participation of large sectors of the Chicano population in places as different as Chicago, Los Angeles, and San Antonio. Raul Ruiz, one of the best-known leaders of La Raza Unida Party in California, commented on this situation as follows:

> In the past, the movement tended to be quite dynamic and energetic in its efforts to protest unjust conditions in this society, but it has also tended to be quite exclusive and elitist.
>
> This is, of course, a criticism, but it is also an observable phenomenon that has affected most movements involved in social struggle, especially in the U.S. (i.e., Panthers, Weathermen).
>
> What I mean by exclusive and elitist is that people have tended to struggle along certain areas of expertise. Thus, we have a myriad of organizations, each doing excellent work but each limited in its scope because of the pre-ordained mission of each organization.[1]

The support and action of the people, not just the militancy of a few activisits, is a requirement which—although present in the movement before La Raza Unida Party—appears today as the most important basis for the political work of a national party.

At the same time, La Raza Unida Party can satisfy the absolute necessity of rescuing Chicanos from the manipulations of the two-party system, especially at election time. After decades of so-called "participation" in the game of choosing between two political parties which represent the same ruling class, Chicanos have seen the possibility of using the electoral process to politicize the people as well as to win certain offices where the Chicano population forms the majority and to win political influence where Chicanos are in the minority.

Since the Depression, the Democratic Party has traditionally counted on winning the Chicano vote. The Kennedy brothers, in particular, knew how to make skillful use of this tendency and it was precisely during the years when the Chicano movement began to grow in strength that the "Viva Kennedy Clubs" were formed. At the same time that the Democrats benefited from Chicano support, they put innumerable obstacles in the way of Chicanos being selected for important Party positions, not only on the national level but also in municipal and state Democratic committees—except where it was known for sure that a "Spanish surname" would be useful—and also that this person would docilely follow the direction of the Democratic bosses. Thanks to the system of primary elections, Democratic leaders were often able to prevent Chicanos who had community support from becoming candidates in the general election. They would withhold party support and financial aid from such candidates.

Another way in which Chicanos were kept under control politically was by the arbitrary division of electoral districts in areas where Chicanos formed the majority. Geographic lines were redrawn so that these majorities could not come together and form an electoral majority.

By these and other means, the two parties in power maintained their monopoly and control over the political life of the country—while at the same time launching big campaigns of rhetoric about their deep concern for the problems of Chicanos. Faced with this situation, La Raza Unida Party hopes to become a political alternative for the thousands of Chicanos who are growing more and more aware of the true motives of the two traditional parties, and of the true class nature of U.S. "democracy." As Raul Ruiz said:

> The Democratic Party and the two-party political system in general has always been abusive of the Chicano community and other Third World communities. We have traditionally been Democrats from generation to generation, because we've seen the Democratic Party as the poor people's party—the party of the working man. But the Democratic Party has been visible in our community only during election time, making promises that they easily forget on election night. . . . In reality, the Democratic Party is in no way different from the Republican Party. Both rely on big business corporations and wealthy individuals with vested interests to supply the monetary contributions to get their candidate elected. Whether a Democrat or Republican is elected, he is still obligated to his financial contributors (who can also assure his reelection) and not to the people whom he supposedly represents.[2]

La Raza Unida Party has developed differently in different areas. But at its best, it is formed and led by the masses of people, together with those students and intellectuals who identify with the masses. It can therefore formulate a platform for struggle that is in accordance not only with the needs and aspirations of Chicanos but also with those of many poor whites and blacks, who also recognize that the present political system is illegitimate and corrupt. This is possible because, as Party spokesmen have pointed out, La Raza Unida Party is not tied up with big business; its obligations are to the interests of the community.

The popular base of La Raza Unida Party does not arise from the existence of identical conditions in all the different Chicano communities. But the Party has succeeded in establishing a minimum of common concerns and common political consciousness, so as to facilitate united and organized action by Chicanos all over the country. This crystallization of certain common denominators is the key to the rise of the Party, and the unusual speed with which it has grown and won political victories in three short years. Nevertheless, this process of crystallization has been far from easy.

The varying conditions of oppression faced by Chicanos throughout their history have produced political positions corresponding to those conditions. For example: police repression has been a constant factor in East Los Angeles, more so than in other regions. As shown in such recent books as *Ando Sangrando* by Armando Morales and *Occupied America* by Rudy Acuña, the last five or six years have seen an intensification of police brutality against Chicanos. (The authors of the present article have also witnessed the repression in East Los Angeles, where the police presence is so massive and frequent, and the police attitude so arrogant toward Chicanos or anyone who "looks" Chicano, that the police forces can truly be called an occupation army in the barrios.) The records of violent incidents kept by such groups as the Community Service Organization and the Council of Mexican-American Affairs make it no exaggeration to say that there is a relationship between the constant repression and the radicalization of Chicanos in East Los Angeles. The political consciousness of Chicanos there has been raised by blows from the billy clubs of the police.

Under such circumstances, it is difficult for those who seek alternatives outside the system to consider taking political positions which imply following the rules of the game—the game from which they not only have been excluded but also have won no gains and much frustration. From this it follows that the electoral form of struggle advocated by La Raza Unida Party met with strong opposition from groups whose political consciousness had developed under the influence of the police violence described above.

In the same way we can understand the position adopted in La Raza Unida Party by Chicanos from Denver, Colorado —a position oriented to tactics of direct confrontation with the power structure. In this case, also, there can be seen a close relationship between the choices of political action and the historic realities of the area, such as the small proportion of Chicanos in Denver (compared to the proportions in other cities of the Southwest), together with a grim socioeconomic situation. These realities have determined the conditions for winning access to power. It is understandable that the fact of being a small minority in the population could lead to confrontation tactics as a means of winning political visibility for Chicanos. This population factor, plus the fact that the Anglo majority's ideology and values are especially aggressive, plus conditions of repression, probably produced a greater need for racial identity and a search for the security of a national Chicano culture.

Within La Raza Unida Party there is a sector influenced by the experiences of Denver, which supports the continuation of tactics used in Colorado and urges that these tactics be adopted by the Party. Other groups in the Party say that the conditions which produced those tactics and made them successful have changed substantially. These groups point to the decline in the struggle for civil rights, and the brutal persecution (and apparent destruction) of the original Black Panther Party.

In September 1972, the first national convention of La Raza Unida Party took place in El Paso, Texas, with about 2,000 delegates from twenty-two states. The convention revealed the variety of tactics which exist. The convention was a landmark; any reference to the development of the Chicano movement must be discussed in terms of "before" or "after" the convention. For those of us who attended as observers, it was of particular political importance to see how a common consciousness had matured, making it possible to mobilize some 2,000 delegates with their own resources and also to lay the foundation for a national party. There was unity among the delegates, based on common conditions of oppression which give them a common enemy. This unity has been expressed in symbols of cultural and national origin that are associated with the common struggle. There was also division among the delegates around questions of tactics. Nevertheless, the importance of the convention was that the forces of unity prevailed—not without a struggle—over the forces of division. A political structure emerged, and also an awareness that the Chicano movement had entered a new phase. Of particular importance was the effort made by leaders from different regions, holding different political positions, to subordinate their personal interests and the feelings of their supporters to the goal of a basic unity in which common interests prevail over differences.

In no way does La Raza Unida Party aim to be a class organization. Ideologically, it cannot be considered a political organization representing the specific interests of a certain social class. Its foundations and ideology are not based on scientific socialism nor on Leninist ideas about the structure and tasks of a party, although some of its leaders have been exposed to Marxist ideas in one form or another.

The political ideology which gave birth to La Raza Unida Party, and which sustains it, is that of nationalism—in its fullest, most progressive, and democratic form, not in the limited, narrow sense of bourgeois nationalism. This ideology, when used in the struggle of national groups or nationalities against oppressor nations, tends to overshadow (or serves when possible to unify) the interests of the different classes within the oppressed group, for the sake of the general interests of the group. However, when a national group exists within the boundaries of another national state—or, as in the case of the Chicanos, when part of the national territory is taken by conquest and annexed to the territory of the other nation—then economic and social relations are established which almost automatically put the great majority of the national group among the dispossessed in the social structure of the dominant nation. Thus most Chicanos face a double exploitation: as members of a colonized national group, and as members of the dispossessed class—the poor. When the national liberation struggle begins in full force, there is the real possibility that any different class interests will overlap so that the national liberation struggle and class interests will become united in their demands and goals.

In the case of La Raza Unida Party, whose members and supporters are overwhelmingly drawn from the most exploited social elements, we see that the Party's actions and political positions—viewed in their own context—have a class perspective. (The same is true of other elements of the movement.) For this reason, José Angel Gutiérrez—founder and present national chairman of the Party—told us in an interview that "the nationalist struggle in the Chicano movement is automatically a class struggle, because we are of the poor."

With this in mind, the Party and many other Chicano organizations make use of a form of nationalism which embraces the different Latin American nationalities. The effects of this in uniting Puerto Ricans, South Americans, Central Americans, and Chicanos will be very important in the near future.

José Angel Gutiérrez told us:

> The dominant ideology of La Raza Unida Party is that ideology which seeks self-determination for the Chicano people, the Latino people, the Hispano people. By Latino and Hispano, I mean people who do not use the term Chicano but who also speak Spanish and are from the countries of the South. La Raza Unida Party includes Puerto Ricans and other Latinos from Central and South America, and it considers them equals—brothers. Another point in our ideology is to establish a nation within the nation. This doesn't mean separatism, but rather that politically, through the electoral and educational process, a way is found to reconquer those parts of the Southwest and the West, wherever there are Chicanos and groups with whom coalitions can be made, and

to conquer the academic, economic, political, and social institutions so that self-determination can be achieved for Chicanos and Latinos.

Another point in our ideology is that we consider ourselves a minority in a colonized situation, like any underdeveloped country. We consider it to be a position of the Party that we are part of the Third World inside the United States.

The Party not only has had a favorable effect on political organizing among Latin Americans who live in the United States. Because of its platform and the very nature of the Party—so different from the politics of the two traditional parties (that "monster with two heads eating from the same plate," as Rodolfo Gonzáles calls them)—it also has attracted a large number of white liberals, students, and professionals. Tired of establishment politics and the economic and social situation in the United States, they see support for the Party as a way of showing their protest and dissatisfaction.

In the November 1972 elections, La Raza Unida Party named as its candidate for governor of Texas a young Chicano lawyer named Ramsey Muñiz. In those sections of Austin with a heavy student population, Muñiz received more votes than either the Republican or Democratic candidate. Although the Democrat won, the Chicano campaign was a success. Raza Unida carried 8 percent of the vote. In Texas, where hatred for the Mexican is almost institutionalized, with monuments, museums, publications, myths, and beliefs that support this hatred, and with decades of Democratic control, that little 8 percent was a triumph and a beginning! The Chicanos had to overcome countless legal obstacles in registering the Party and during the entire electoral process. All types of fraud were committed against the Party: stealing ballots, closing the voting booths five hours before the official hour in areas where there was a heavy Chicano population, etc. The Party also faced a hostile press, which put up walls of silence around pro-Party activities. All means were used to brush away the victory represented by the fact that, as a result of the 1972 elections, the Party will automatically be on the ballot in the 1974 elections. Those means included direct repression by the police and the hated Texas Rangers (called "rinches" by Chicanos) and the jailing of several Party leaders. Nevertheless, as José Angel told us, "the candidacy of Muñiz undoubtedly did a great deal to develop the positive image of a powerful and viable party."

Despite its triumphs and the great experience which the Party has had in Texas (the area best known to the authors of this article), it is still in the stage of organization and consolidation. There are still ideological conflicts, problems of opportunism, regionalism, and a lack of unity among leaders. These conflicts have certainly created division at the present time and may continue to do so for a while. But these very conflicts are producing much needed discussion of long-range Chicano goals and the meaning of nationalism, as well as discussion of leadership methods. The Party may or may not become the final tool for mass organization of Mexicanos, but it is playing a vital historical role.

Notes

1. Raul Ruiz, "El Partido de La Raza Unida," in *La Raza*, no. 7 (January 1972).
2. Ibid.

9

The Black Berets'
Twelve-Point Program

*The beret has become a symbol of Chicano militancy,
especially among the youth and especially in urban areas.
The first group of Brown Berets was organized in Los
Angeles in 1967; their activities included protesting racism in
the school system, exposing and combatting police brutality,
publishing a newspaper, and opening a clinic to serve people
in the barrio. Since then, many Chicano groups that wear
either brown or black berets have been formed across the
country. All of them have placed emphasis on service to the
community and a refusal to compromise with basic principles. Here is the twelve-point platform adopted by Las
Gorras Negras, the Black Beret organization of Albuquerque, New Mexico, in 1970.*

We, the members of the Black Berets of Albuquerque,
Aztlán, being aware of the injustices, discriminatory, and
oppressive actions against La Raza, hereby pledge to commit
our lives to the SERVICE, EDUCATION, AND DE-
FENSE of La Santa Raza.

In order to combat injustices, racial discrimination, and

Reprinted from *Venceremos*, the newspaper of the Black Beret organization, Albuquerque 1971.

oppression we have set up a defense against the repressive agencies which carry out these established practices against the Chicano and all Third World peoples. To have an effective defense against these practices we must observe at all times the federal, state, local, and other agencies which are the main contributors to the repressive conditions which exist among La Raza and all other Third World peoples.

To serve the people means not only to correct the injustices, but to provide, wherever necessary, the necessities for a complete humane society. Whatever these necessities might be, a Black Beret will do everything within his power to provide them. We realize that to save our people we must be motivated, not only by the hatred for the *marrano racista*, but by the great emotions and feelings of love that we have for our Raza and the Third World peoples.

We have come to the conclusion that we cannot solve the total problems by ourselves so one of our most important tasks is to make our people aware. This is education. In order to completely educate people we must not only concentrate on the problems and the causes, but we must instill in our people pride in our culture and heritage and love for that which is ours.

THEREFORE THE BLACK BERETS' DUTY IS TO SERVE, EDUCATE, AND DEFEND.

1. WE WANT SELF-DETERMINATION AND LIBERATION FOR ALL THE CHICANOS IN THE U.S.A.

Before the Amerikkkans came into being we were here in the Southwest. When they came we taught them how to survive in the Southwest. Yet they have cheated, killed, and exploited us. Now the time has come to stop all this. We demand control over our own destinies and the power be placed in the hands of the Chicano people in order to make AZTLÁN a reality and to insure our future existence. QUE VIVA AZTLÁN LIBRE!

2. WE WANT SELF-DETERMINATION FOR ALL LATINOS AND THIRD WORLD PEOPLES.

We will not be free until our Puerto Rican, Black, Indian, and Asian brothers in the U.S.A. are also free from the oppressive and colonial rule of this system. We are not free until our brothers in Latin America, Africa, and Asia are liberated. Our struggles are basically the same. We must unite to end discrimination, injustices and to rise out of poverty. NO CHICANO IS FREE UNTIL ALL OPPRESSED PEOPLE ARE FREE!

3. WE WANT COMMUNITY CONTROL OF OUR INSTITUTIONS AND LAND.

We want control of our communities by our people and programs to guarantee that all institutions serve the needs of our people. People's control of Police, Health Services, Churches, Schools, Housing, Transportation and Welfare are needed. We want an end to attacks on our Land by urban renewal, highway destruction, universities, and corporations. LA TIERRA ES DE LA GENTE!

4. WE WANT A TRUE EDUCATION OF OUR MESTIZO CULTURE AND SPANISH LANGUAGE.

We want an end to the cultural genocide perpetuated by the Amerikkkan educational system against Chicanos. We must be taught about our ancestors truthfully. Pancho Villa and Zapata were revolutionaries, not bandits. Spanish is our language and must be taught as so. Our culture, a revolutionary culture, is the only true teaching. VIVA NUESTRA CULTURA MESTIZA!

5. WE WANT FREEDOM FOR ALL POLITICAL PRISONERS.

ALL CHICANOS must be freed since they have been tried by racist courts and not by their own people. We want all freedom fighters released from jail. FREE TIJERINA AHORA!

6. WE OPPOSE THE AMERIKKKAN MILITARY AND ITS UNJUST WARS OF OPPRESSION.
We want the U.S.A. out of Vietnam and LATIN AMERICA and the oppressed communities of the U.S.A. CHICANOS should not serve in the Amerikkkan armed services, since they are denied the right to live with dignity and pride here in the U.S.A. U.S.A. OUT OF VIETNAM, LATIN AMERICA, AND AZTLÁN!

7. WE WANT EQUALITY FOR WOMEN. MACHISMO MUST BE REVOLUTIONARY . . . NOT OPPRESSIVE.
Under this system our women have been oppressed both by the system and our men. The doctrine of Machismo has been used by our men to take out their frustrations on their wives, sisters, mothers, and children. We must support our women in their struggle for economic and social equality and recognize that our women are equals within our struggle for Liberation. FORWARD HERMANAS IN THE STRUGGLE!

8. WE WANT AN IMMEDIATE END TO POLICE HARASSMENT, BRUTALITY, AND MURDER OF LA RAZA.
For years the colonizing army in our barrios, the police, have been beating, killing, and imprisoning our RAZA. The police must stop now and not tomorrow. They must realize that they can jail us, beat us, and kill us, but they will never stop our determination to be free. We demand community control of the Police. END POLICE BRUTALITY NOW!!!

9. WE WANT FOR OUR PEOPLE TO HAVE THE BASIC NECESSITIES TO EXIST.

We want for our people to be given the things necessary for existence, such as decent housing, clothing, food, transportation and medical services. Luxuries are privileges that must be paid for, but a man has the basic rights to have a roof over his head, to have food and clothes for him and his family, to good health, and transportation wherever he has to go. We DEMAND that the people receive all this from the Amerikkkan government as is their RIGHT. ¡HASTA LA VICTORIA SIEMPRE!

10. WE WANT FULL EMPLOYMENT FOR OUR PEOPLE.

We believe that the federal government is responsible and obligated to give every man employment and a guaranteed income. We believe that if the white Amerikkkan businessman will not give full employment, then the means of production should be taken from the businessman and placed in the community so that the people in the community can organize and employ all of its people and give a high standard of living. NO MORE UNEMPLOYMENT!

11. WE OPPOSE CAPITALISM AND ALLIANCES MADE BY OUR TREACHEROUS POLITICOS.

We oppose the politicos which oppress our people and give us empty promises before elections. We oppose the poverty pimps which keep our people down through useless and stagnated programs, social workers which keep our barrios divided and brothers fighting each other for crumbs. These people keep us from achieving our freedom. We demand that the people be given control of their barrios through political and economic power. ¡VENCEREMOS!

12. WE BELIEVE ARMED SELF-DEFENSE AND

ARMED STRUGGLE ARE THE ONLY MEANS TO LIBERATION.

We are against violence, the violence of illiteracy, the violence of hungry children, the violence of diseased old people, and the violence of poverty and profit. We have gone to the courts to protest racism and discrimination, we have voted for the politicos who have given us empty promises, we have demonstrated peacefully for what we believe in only to be met with more violence, injustices, and discrimination. We have to arm ourselves now to protect ourselves and the people from the oppression perpetuated by the businessmen, government, and police. When a government oppresses our people, we have the right to abolish it and create a new one. EL CHICANO HA DESPERTADO! CUIDATE CHOTA!

10

La Chicana:
The Brown Woman
and Today's Struggle

*Like other Third World or non-white women, the Chicana
suffers from what some have called triple oppression. In
addition to the racism and exploitation that all of La Raza
face, she faces also a third enemy, oppression based on the
fact that she was born a woman—oppression in the form of
sexism. The "woman question," as it is often called in the
Chicano movement, has been and continues to be a subject
of much debate. The following two articles present the most
often heard positions on that question. Neither expresses the
totally feminist position, today held by a small minority of
Chicanas.*

La Chicana, the Chicano Movement,
and Women's Liberation

Contrary to the concern of many Chicanos, the women's
liberation movement seems to hold little or no appeal for the
majority of Chicanas on the university campus. This seems to

The first of these articles originally appeared in the *Chicano Studies
Newsletter* and is reprinted from *El Chicano*, April 30, 1971; the second
was published in *Pamoja Venceremos*. Both are California publications.

be true particularly in the case of Chicanas who have been involved, even in a minimal way, with the contemporary thrust of "El Movimiento." These same Chicanas are, nevertheless, beginning to understand the potential their collective influence could have for the Chicanada. This article is written in an effort to outline some of the major differences between Chicanas and white women liberationists and to provoke the focus for the course, "La Chicana," offered by Chicano Studies this spring.

There are major philosophical and tactical differences between Chicanas and white women's liberation groups. Neither of the two factions of the women's movement addresses itself totally to the issues central to the concern of the Chicana. The most obvious discrepancy lies in the very concept of a women's movement as an independent force for social change. In the United States there is no qualitative difference between the social experience of the Chicana and the Chicano. That is not true in the case of white women and white men. In American society, white men have a distinct advantage and have used that advantage to limit and shape the lives of women with the same apparent lack of conscience with which they oppress racial minorities. It makes sense for white women to struggle against the controlling influence of white men just as it makes sense for Chicanos and Chicanas to struggle together against the forces of racism and economic exploitation that deny them the basic human right to self-determination.

This is not to say that Chicanas cannot identify with some aspects of the white women's struggle for equality. They can and do. Educational and professional freedom is a major issue among the more moderate faction of the white women's movement. Likewise, most Chicanas will tell you women should have equal access to higher education in whatever field of endeavor that interests them. That means that if women want to become architects, engineers or neurosurgeons, they should not be frustrated in that pursuit.

At the same time, Chicanas understand that most Chicanos spend no more than eight years in school. Educational opportunity has been systematically denied to all of our people, not just our women. None of the predominantly white, middle-class, professional women's groups have come to grips with racism in American society or the deliberate role of the government in the oppression of Chicano people educationally and in every other way. These women are reformists in the liberal tradition. As a force for change, they are basically irrelevant to the Chicano people and therefore to Chicanas.

The radical faction of women's liberation does address itself precisely to the social, economic and political conditions that happen to oppressed white women in some of the ways Third World people have been oppressed ever since white men and women set foot on the Americas. Unfortunately, many of these women focus on the maleness of our present social system as though, by implication, a female-dominated white America would have taken a more reasonable course. Chicanas have no more faith in white women than in white men. We are oppressed by a system that serves white power and depends upon a white majority for its survival and perpetuation. In our struggles we identify our men, not white women, as our natural allies.

That we have decided as Chicanas that our place is beside our men and with each other does not mean there are no problems between us or that we as women are completely satisfied in our relationship to our men. Many Chicanas feel a deep sense of frustration over the fact that so many Chicanos perceive us in roles limited more by romantic conceptions of the past and of our grandmothers before us than by historical reality. In fact, the women of La Raza have always shared the lot of their men, and since the time of first contact with white Western society, that lot has been a difficult one demanding the sacrifices of our women as well as our men. The struggles we face today will require no less.

On the Brown Women's Struggle!
*Statement from the Brown Women's
Venceremos Collective*

Venceremos supports no separatist movements on any level. While at the same time recognizing the initial importance of the women's struggle, the success of the revolution, of our fight to eliminate political, economic and social injustices, will depend on equal efforts. Women are one half and the men the other half. Neither can win without the other.

Our Vietnamese sisters have set down a revolutionary example of the women's role in the revolution. There is no place for individualism on any level in the fight to defeat U.S. imperialism. Men and women are fighting side by side. Their struggles are equal and dependent on each other. There is no place for male chauvinism. Women should be strong and men need to respect their strength, and should not try to force them back into weaker roles.

It is very important that we understand the women's struggle as part of an overall struggle toward a socialist society and not a separate struggle that should take priority.

We demand and must continue to struggle for a society where equal rights and respect for women as whole human beings are practiced. That means an end to discrimination within industry, educational institutions, the home, the mass media, and in everyday social life.

The history of the brown woman shows us that her role has been a very strong one. Wherever she has seen the suffering of her people, she has responded bravely, with total commitment. We, as the women of La Raza, must dare to carry on the revolutionary tradition of las Adelitas, who fought so courageously during the Mexican Revolution.

In the case of the Chicana and other brown women, however, this role has often been a silent one. Because of the high unemployment rate among brown men, brown women have often been placed in the difficult role of being both mother and father to her children. She must then face not only racist bosses in her work, but also many household and child care burdens. Child care is one of the most difficult problems for a woman to face alone. She is troubled with having to leave a good part of the raising of her children to others, because she wants the best care for them. But we must understand exactly what la Familia de la Raza means. It means we must trust each other and make the care of our children truly a collective responsibility. We must combat all this society's ideas about the family which tell us that children are the private property of the parents. The Raza movement is based on brother and sisterhood. We must look at each other as one large family. We must look at all the children as belonging to all of us.

The development of day care centers for children puts into practice these ideas. The Venceremos child care center in Redwood City is one such center.

A woman who has no way of expressing herself and of realizing herself as a full human being has nothing else to turn to but the owning of material things. She builds her entire life around these, and finds security in this way. All she has to live for is her house and family; she becomes very possessive of both. This makes her totally dependent on her husband and family. Often a brown woman who feels that this position is "comfortable" does not become a part of the movement for social justice. Many times her fears about becoming involved are caused by fears of how her husband, family, and friends will respond. Often her husband will not recognize the real source of his problems (the economic system itself), but will instead come home and take it out on his family. The brown woman who sees her true responsibility not only to her family but to all of her people, has many difficulties to face. Only the will and determination to serve our people which is our heritage, can overcome these difficulties.

We feel that every woman has the right to practice whatever birth control measures that she chooses. But many women, especially Third World women, are misinformed about such methods. Each woman has an absolute right to correct information about her own physical and emotional needs. No one, from social workers to husbands, has the right to make a woman feel guilty about not wanting a child at a particular time in her life. In all cases, the decision must be her own.

Yet many times, brown women are coerced or forced not to have children. We as brown women must have the will to struggle for our own childrens' survival while the ruling class is still oppressing us. Only this kind of strong determination to live can combat the propaganda. While often directly genocidal, it is sometimes written by ignorant, though well-intentioned, people, who do not understand the issues of our struggle as colonized peoples. It tries to tell us that we are depriving our children of necessary food, clothing, and housing; that in order to survive, we must stop bearing children. We would like to make very clear that *we* are not and have never been responsible for that deprivation. Under this system of capitalism, we are not the ones who decide what kind of food, clothing, and housing our people get. The same applies to all working people, those who built this country, who labor in the fields and factories, do not have any control over how products are made or how resources are distributed. Politically, the only "power" working-class people have is to vote on which politicians will continue to serve the interests of the ruling class who then go on maintaining total control.

It is to end such economic and political oppression that we involve ourselves in revolutionary struggle against these forces which *are* responsible. In order to do this, we need as many brown babies as possible growing up to carry on our revolutionary task.

Only in a society based on cooperation and run by the masses of working people will it be possible for things to be different. Even then it will take a long time to get rid of such incorrect ideas about women being "inferior" to men. We must begin now to attack those ideas and to struggle to change the ways men and women relate. Revolutionaries, especially, and those who are trying to become revolutionaries, must live up to the idea of men and women being equal. Revolutionary men have a special responsibility to bring these ideas to the men they are working with.

Some white women who recognize the importance of the women's struggle have begun to reject their roles in the social and political struggles going on in this country. The brown woman, the Third World woman, has no such choice. She is, out of necessity, but more so out of love, unavoidably bound to all her people. She cannot only concern herself with her oppression as a woman, for she shares in common this system's racist oppression with the rest of her Raza.

Women being equal also means women taking seriously their responsibility to defend themselves, their children, and the rest of their people. We must be willing to defend our lives and our rights whenever they come under attack—by any means necessary. This means developing the needed skills in order to do so. We know the bosses, the politicians, the police, don't give up anything without a fight. We can only win if we gather together all our forces, women and men, to fight our enemy on every level. And in defeating our real enemy—U.S. capitalism and imperialism—we, as Third World women, will find our true liberation.

11

Chicano Prisoners Speak Out:
Two Letters and an Exchange of Poems

One of the most striking aspects of the Chicano movement in recent years has been the growing strength of Los Pintos, Chicanos in prison. Behind bars, they have been forming organizations, publishing newsletters, holding art shows, and carrying out many activities to assert their new spirit of Chicanismo, revealing a high political consciousness—as can be seen from the following letters.

I am writing this letter on behalf of the carnales here with me in this prison. We are in a place in the prison known as the "hole." We wish to extend at this time our love, respect, and admiration to all the carnalas y carnales in the struggle for our Raza. This also extends to all who are involved in the struggle against oppression, poverty, police brutality, and all the social ills that we are faced with today in society. Whether in prison or out there on the streets, we love each and everyone involved in this wanting justice and freedom for all who are enslaved in this world. They may have our bodies here in prison but they will never imprison our minds! There have been too many murders of our Raza and these deaths cannot be allowed to be in vain now or ever!

These letters and poems originally appeared in *El Grito del Norte* in September, October, and April 1972, and are reprinted with permission.

On behalf of all the families that have lost loved ones in the struggle we send our condolences but each of you must remember now and forever that these were dedicated soldiers who were unselfish and had a love for their Raza that knew no bounds for all of us! The men and women who have died so far are all with God in Heaven now!

We must continue where these soldiers left off because if we don't, then we are traitors who have cheated these brave soldiers in death! But we are not traitors nor weaklings so we shall continue the struggle until we have overcome or there is no more Raza! As long as we are alive, let us all fight no matter what hardships we must endure for we shall overcome this system not only for ourselves but for our children and the future generations to come!

We, the Pintos, will do all we can for our Raza, for we don't fear death. We want equality for all and not just the rich! If death comes to one of us, we will meet it with a smile and our death will not be in vain as we know in our hearts that our people would never allow this!

> Con amor y respeto a mi linda raza.
> De parte de todos los soldados
> aquí en California que se encuen-
> tran en los hoyos de la pinta.

> Juan Santoya, "El Triste"
> Tracy, California

Camaradas, carnales y carnalas:

I can speak for my carnales and myself here at this $17,000,000 ultramodern prison complex, where our people are kept in an unhuman fashion, thousands of miles from our homes. I say this because we are socialists and because we have chosen to pursue the very basic socialistic standards by which to conduct our daily lives in this so-called penitentiary. We find ourselves being constantly abused by our keepers, because of our political beliefs. And, like others throughout this country, *we too have awakened from the long capitalist addiction-type sleep of unawareness, to find ourselves political prisoners in this land that belongs to the people.*

We feel that we don't suffer from this type of treatment that we are receiving, as they would like. Rather than that, like a good wine placed in cellar, we have developed into something quite different and rather remarkable as a result of being victims of time and brutality. El movimiento de nuestra raza es una lucha that has long been protracted and is finally taking shape in the forming of the long-awaited union.

The eleventh hour of nuestra raza is coming into view. Each of us knows the things that must be done (why, when and how). We have seen what steps our enemy will take, as they did with our carnales Antonio Cordova, Rito Canales and countless others. We know the pigs are consistent in their methods of taking us off one by one. We must ready ourselves.

The thing that must remain paramount is LA CAUSA. Sacrifice and dedication—we cannot waver from these responsibilities. Libertad para todos prisioneros politicos!

Victor Gerardo Boño*

A major event in raising the political consciousness of Chicano prisoners was the police assassination of Antonio Cordova and Rito Canales in Albuquerque, New Mexico, on January 29, 1972. Rito was himself an ex-convict, working to improve conditions in the prison he had left. Antonio Cordova, who also came from a poor Chicano family, was a

---

* Victor Boño is in the hole at the federal prison in Marion, Illinois. He was originally sentenced in California for the killing of two federal officers in 1967.

reporter and photographer for the Chicano movement press. When killed, he was working to expose prison conditions and police brutality.

Before his death, Antonio Cordova wrote a poem to Luis Talamantez—probably the best-known Chicano political prisoner in the country. After the assassination, Luis Talamantez wrote a poem for the two dead brothers. This exchange reflects the growing solidarity felt between Chicanos behind walls and those outside.

For Talamantez
by Antonio Cordova

Talamantez! TALAMANTEZ!
Are you there?
    Yes, you dirty bastards I'm
Still here!
    And the fading footsteps echo
Thru the hollow shell,
    A cold and empty cell.

Talamantez! TALAMANTEZ!
We will break you—soon or late
    The body is easily broken, but
the spirit is too great!
    And the days slip in and out
of that dark and barren shell,
    A cold and empty cell.

Talamantez! TALAMANTEZ!
In darkness, what do you see?
    Guns with which you hold Aztlán,
And jails you keep us in, but

though we're wrapped in chains
The jailer is not free!
   And the hollow ring of steel on
Steel echoes thru that barren shell,
   A cold and empty cell.

   Talamantez! TALAMANTEZ!
Your lost youth will never be
   Regained.
   True, the hair grows white, but
In the process I have learned the
   Way you think—I have learned
Your language, your politics, your
   Strengths and your weaknesses.
I have learned the enemy!
   In keeping me here, what have you
Gained?
   And the years creep in and out of
That dark, repressive shell,
   A cold and empty cell.

   Talamantez! TALAMANTEZ!
Free, you shall NEVER be!
   When the Eagle finds the Serpent,
We shall see!
   And a nervous laughter echoed
Thru that hollow shell,
   A cold and empty cell.

   Talamantez! TALAMANTEZ!
Are you there?
      Are you there?
         ARE YOU THERE?
   And the words re-echoed thru
That dark, forbidding shell,
   A cold and empty cell.

Para Antonio y Rito
por Luis Talamantez

Dedicado a mis hermanos de sal y sangre,
Antonio Cordova y Rito Canales, soldados
de la gente

Epáh, manos!
Antonio/Rito,
Su gente oyó su ultimo grito
como hombres de su Raza
enteros se dieron
y en espiritu grande—asi murieron
        . . . asi pasó . . .

Antonio/Rito
su pueblo los han perdido
pero nuestra causa se avanzó,
y la tierra en donde han dado la vida,
esa se libertó
porque la sangre suyas
Aztlán allí se la tomó,
        . . . se la tomó.

Adios—
Antonio/ahora quien sabe en donde estes,
y Rito/moristes por primera y última vez,
hermanos!
La Raza está hecha
por sacrificantes como ustedes
si allá/en el mero masalla se sienten,
nunca se sienten
que fue por nada—nunca repienten!
muera el cochi—
y viva, viva La Raza, la gente.

For Antonio and Rito
by Luis Talamantez

Dedicated to my brothers de sal y sangre (salt and blood),
Antonio Cordova and Rito Canales,
soldiers of the people

Epah! brothers!
Antonio/Rito
Your people heard your last outcry
as men of your Raza
wholly you gave yourselves
and with great spirit—thus you died
        . . . thus it happened . . .

Antonio/Rito
you have been lost to your people
but our cause advanced,
and the land where you gave your lives
was freed
when Aztlán, on that spot,
took your blood, drank it in,
        . . . drank it in.

Farewell—
Antonio/who knows now where you are?
And Rito/you died for the first and last time
Brothers!
La Raza is made
from those who sacrifice, like you,
if there, in some "faraway," you are feeling,
and if, at the moment of death, sorrow was felt,
then never feel it was for nothing—never regret!
      Death to the pig—
      and live, long live La Raza and the people.

Bilingual Bibliography

Books

Acuña, Rudy. *A Mexican American Struggle*. New York: American Book Co., 1971.

————. *Occupied America: The Chicano Struggle for Liberation*. New York: Harper & Row, 1972.

Aguilar, Alonso. *Pan-Americanism: From Monroe to the Present*. New York: Monthly Review Press, 1968.

Akzin, Benjamin. *Estado y nación*. Mexico: Fondo de Cultura Económica, 1968.

Alcaraz, Ramón, ed. *Apuntes para la historia de la guerra entre Mexico y los Estados Unidos*. Mexico: Siglo XXI, 1970.

Balenki, A. *La intervención extranjera en México, 1861–1867*. Mexico: Fondo de Cultura Popular, 1966.

Barrett, D. N. "Demographic Characteristics." *La Raza. Forgotten Americans*. Edited by Julián Samora. Notre Dame, Ind.: University of Notre Dame Press, 1966.

Belliaeff, A. *Understanding the Mexican American in Today's Culture*. San Diego, Cal.: San Diego Project, 1966.

Burma, John H. *Spanish-Speaking Groups in the United States*. Durham, N.C.: Duke University Press, 1954.

Cánovas, A. *Historia social y los Estados Unidos de América*. Mexico: Ed. Jus., 1962.

Carreño, Alberto María. *La diplomacia extraordinaria entre México y los Estados Unidos, 1789–1947*. 2 vols. Mexico: Ed. Jus., 1951.

184   *The Chicanos*

Carreño, Alberto María. *México y los Estados Unidos de América.* Mexico: Ed. Jus., 1962.

Clark, Kenneth. *Dark Ghetto: Dilemmas of Social Power.* New York: Harper & Row, 1965.

Clark, Margaret. *Health in the Mexican-American Culture: A Community Study.* Berkeley and Los Angeles: University of California Press, 1959.

Clendenen, C. C. *Blood on the Border.* New York: Macmillan Co., 1969.

Dunne, John G. *Delano.* New York: Farrar, Straus & Giroux, 1971.

Estados Unidos ante su Crisis. Mexico: Siglo XXI, 1967.

Fogel, Walter. *Mexican-Americans in Southwest Labor Markets.* Advance Report 10. Los Angeles: Mexican-American Study Project, 1967.

Fuentes Díaz, Vicente. *La intervención norteaméricana en México, 1847.* Mexico: 1947.

Fusco, P., and Horwitz, G. *La Causa: The California Grape Strike.* New York: Macmillan Co., 1970.

Galarza, Ernesto. *Merchants of Labor: The Mexican Bracero Story.* Santa Barbara, Cal.: McNally and Loftin, 1966.

—————. *Spiders in the House and Workers in the Field.* Notre Dame, Ind.: University of Notre Dame Press, 1970.

—————, Gallegos, H., and Samora, J. *Mexican-Americans in the Southwest.* Santa Barbara, Cal.: McNally and Loftin, 1970.

Gamio, Manuel. *Mexican Immigration to the United States.* Chicago: University of Chicago Press, 1930.

Gill, M. *Nuestros buenos vecinos.* Mexico: Ed. Azteca, 1959.

Goldfinch, Charles W. *Juan N. Cortina, 1824–1892: A Reappraisal.* Brownsville, Tex.: Bishop's Print Shop, 1950.

González, Nancie. *The Spanish-Americans of New Mexico: A Heritage of Pride.* Albuquerque, N. Mex.: University of New Mexico Press, 1969.

Grebler, Leo. *Mexican Immigration to the United States: The Record and Its Implication.* Advance Report 2. Los Angeles: Mexican-American Study Project, 1966.

—————, Moore, Joan, and Guzman, Ralph. *The Mexican-American People: The Nation's Second Largest Minority.* New York: Free Press, 1971.

Guerra y Sanchez, Ramiro. *La expansión territorial de los Estados Unidos*. Havana: Ed. National, 1964.

Handlin, Oscar. *Race and Nationality in American Life*. Boston: Little, Brown, 1957.

Heller, Celia S. *Mexican-American Youth: Forgotten Youth at the Crossroads*. New York: Random House, 1966.

López, M. *Economia y politica en la historia de México*. Mexico: Ed. Solidaridad, 1965.

Madsen, William. *Mexican-Americans of South Texas*. New York: Holt, Rinehart and Winston, 1964.

Matthiessen, P. *Sal si Puedes—Escape If You Can: César Chávez and the New American Revolution*. New York: Random House, 1970.

McWilliams, Carey. *Brothers Under the Skin*. Boston: Brown and Co., 1948.

————. *Factories in the Field*. 3rd ed. Hamden, Conn.: Shoe String Press, 1969.

————. *Mexicans in America*. Edited by Clifford L. Lord. New York: Teachers' College Press, 1970.

————. *North from Mexico*. 1942; reprint ed. Westport, Conn.: Greenwood Press, 1968.

Medina Castro, Manuel. *Estados Unidos de norteamérica y América Latina en el Siglo XIX*. Havana: Casa de las Americas, 1968.

Merk, Frederick. *Manifest Destiny and Mission in American History*. New York: Knopf, 1963.

Mittlebach, Frank, and Marshall, Grace. *The Burden of Poverty*. Advance Report 5. Los Angeles: Mexican-American Study Project, 1966.

Moore, Joan W. *Mexican-Americans: Problems and Prospects*. Madison, Wis.: University of Wisconsin Press, 1967.

————, and Mittlebach, Frank. *Residential Segregation in the Urban Southwest*. Advance Report 4. Los Angeles: Mexican-American Study Project, 1966.

Moquin, Wayne, ed. *A Documentary History of the Mexican-American*. New York: Praeger, 1971.

Morín, Raul. *Among the Valiant*. Alhambra, Cal.: Borden, 1963.

Nabokov, Peter. *Tijerina and the Courthouse Raid*. Berkeley, Cal.: Ramparts Press, Inc., 1971.

Now. Havana: Instituto del Libro, 1967.

Paredes, Américo. *With His Pistol in His Hand.* Austin, Tex.: University of Texas Press, 1958.

————, and Paredes, Raymund. *Mexican-American Authors.* Boston: Houghton Mifflin, 1971.

Peón, Maximo. *Cómo viven los mexicanos en Estados Unidos.* Mexico: Costa-Amic., 1966.

Polk, James. *The Diary of a President, 1845–1849.* Edited by Allan Nevins. New York: G. P. Putnam, 1968.

Rendon, Armando B. *Chicano Manifesto.* New York: Macmillan Co., 1971.

Robles, H. *Los desarraigados.* Mexico: INBA, 1962.

Rose, Peter I. *They and We: Racial and Ethnic Relations in the United States.* New York: Random House, 1964.

Rubel, Arthur J. *Across the Tracks: Mexican-Americans in a Texas City.* Austin, Tex.: University of Texas Press, 1966.

Simmen, Edward, ed. *The Chicano: From Caricature to Self-Portrait.* New York: New American Library, 1971.

Simpson, George E., and Yinger, J. Milton. *Racial and Cultural Minorities.* New York: Harper & Row, 1953.

Stalin, Joseph V. *Selected Works.* Davis, Cal.: Cardinal, 1971.

Steiner, Stan. *La Raza. The Mexican-Americans.* New York: Harper & Row, 1970.

Trueba, A. *California, tierra perdida.* 2 vols. Mexico: Ed. Jus., 1967.

Trujilla, R. *Olvídate de Alamo.* Mexico: La Prensa, 1965.

Watson, J. *The Structure of Discontent.* Los Angeles: University of California Press, 1967.

Vásquez, Richard. *Chicano.* Garden City, N. Y.: Doubleday, 1970.

Vásquez de Knauth, Josefina. *Mexicanos y norteaméricanos ante la guerra de 47.* Mexico: SepSetentas, 1972.

Articles

"Cuadernos de Poder Negro." *Marcha* (Montevideo), no. 12 (1968). "Reyes Lopéz Tijerina." *Tiempo* (Mexico) LIII, no. 1365 (July 1968).

"Los Mexicanos en busca de una identidad." *The Economist para America Latina* (Mexico), June 12, 1968.

Romano, O. "Charismatic Medicine: Folk-Healing and Folk-Saint-hood." *American Anthropologist* 67, no. 5 (1960), pt. 1.

——————. "Donshipin. A Mexican-American Community in Texas." *American Anthropologist* 62, no. 6 (1960).

Documents and Census

A Badge of Infamy: A Petition to the United Nations on the Treatment of the Mexican Immigrant. New York: American Committee for the Protection of the Foreign Born, 1959.

Among the Spanish-Americans. Testimony presented at the Cabinet Committee Hearings on Mexican-American Affairs. El Paso, Texas, October 26–28, 1967.

Colegio Jacinto Treviño. Pamphlet prepared for the Committee of Public Relations of Mercedes community. 1971.

Spanish Surnamed American Employment in the Southwest. Greeley, Col.: Colorado Civil Rights Commission, 1970.

U.S., Bureau of the Census. *Current Population Report*, Series P-20, nos. 213 (February 1971), and 238 (July 1972).

U.S., Department of Commerce. *Census of Population.* Persons of Spanish Surnames and Non-White Population by Race. 1960.

——————. *General Population Characteristics.* Advanced Report PC(V2) -I. 1971.